WALKING Is OVERRATED

Witnessing the World from Two Perspectives

Michael R. Maruzzi

ISBN 979-8-88644-490-2 (Paperback)
ISBN 979-8-88644-491-9 (Digital)

Copyright © 2023 Michael R. Maruzzi
All rights reserved
First Edition

All rights reserved. No part of this publication may be reproduced, distributed, or transmitted in any form or by any means, including photocopying, recording, or other electronic or mechanical methods without the prior written permission of the publisher. For permission requests, solicit the publisher via the address below.

Covenant Books
11661 Hwy 707
Murrells Inlet, SC 29576
www.covenantbooks.com

CONTENTS

ACKNOWLEDGMENT

This personal accomplishment would never have been possible if not for the support of my family, most especially my mother and father, Diane and Robert Maruzzi; my wife, Arlene; my sister, Sandra; and the rest of my loving family, both old and new.

Katelin and Michael: You have been my inspiration and will continue to be for the rest of my life.

Sonny, Micayla, Janel, and Pasquale: Thank you for sharing your mother and your children with me.

Jeff, my "first wife:" I am so grateful for everything that you have brought to my life. I love you, brother.

Finally, I would like to thank my friend, Paul, for marrying such a wonderful and intelligent woman. Stacy, my editor, your friendship and help with this book are appreciated so much more than you will ever know.

FOREWORD

Tuesday, October 18, 2022

Laying on my belly to relieve three pressure wounds on my backside, I've had the same, isolated view out my hospital window for the past six weeks. There is one palm tree in my sightline. It once was filled with leaves, but after the hurricane, there are two remaining. Those couple palm leaves fluttering in a nice breeze against the beautiful blue sky give me hope. I cannot wait for seven days to pass. I use 'seven days' loosely, because there have been two or three occasions that I thought I might be going home. This one seems fairly concrete. It will be my first opportunity in a while to have more than just a view of the sunshine outside. The weather since Hurricane Ian has been almost perfect—just my luck that I've been indoors.

Sunshine is probably the greatest driving force in my life. I get a burst of energy and motivation on sunny mornings. The instant I am in my wheelchair, I head outside to find the perfect spot to tilt back and feel the warmth on my face. My entire body and mind relax, which is deeply satisfying to me. It is the one moment during my day that I get to focus on life above my neck, the only part of my body that I physically control. I lay back, grateful for the moment. The break from my body makes me feel life is still worth living and worth living well!

My life is made up of moments, good and bad. Each moment linked together has shaped the course of my life. Living as a quadriplegic, I have learned that, so often, we hold on to the past instead of focusing on the most important moment: the next one.

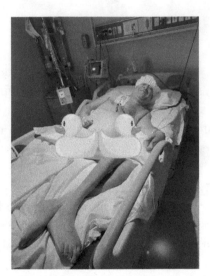

October 2022. 'Spa Day' at the hospital. Here's a little bit of eye candy for you. Getting my hair washed for the first time in a month felt so good. I was fighting through valleys of depression, and this treat was just enough to change my mindset. I invested in these moments of positivity, like how each morning, I was awakened by people lifting up the sheet to look at my recently repaired rear end. "How does it look?" I would ask. The response was always, "Everything looks great." Having so many people admiring my derriere made me feel a bit like a supermodel.

CHAPTER 1

Hurricane Ian

Tuesday, September 27, 2022
Fort Myers, Florida

"One roll forward. Two rolls back." I am taking liberty with a popular sentiment to make it more wheelchair accessible. The phrase seems an appropriate representation of the events of my life over the last several months. As I write this, I am laying in the hallway at Lee Memorial Hospital in Fort Myers, Florida. Hurricane Ian, a category five hurricane, is blowing by outside, and all the patients have been moved into the hallway, away from windows, in case flying debris crashes into our rooms. I am on the fourth floor, and one of the nurses jokes that she thought she saw an alligator fly by. Though it didn't really happen, it's not out of the realm of possibilities with wind speeds as high as 155 miles per hour.

How did I get here? A summertime that started with such joy and promise quickly reversed course and turned my life upside down. The story begins four months ago when my wife, Arlene, and I traveled up to Massachusetts. On May twenty-first, we celebrated the birth of our seventh grandchild, Genaro, and we attended a family wedding on Memorial Day weekend. Four days later, I tested positive for COVID-19. I am considered 'very high risk' as a quadriplegic, so I ended up in the hospital. While there, I developed a pressure wound. A CAT scan later discovered second and third pressure wounds, one

1

seven centimeters deep, going right up to my pelvic bone. Now, a bone infection became concerning. I received four days of treatment to help with my breathing and wound care and was released from the hospital on the fifth day.

At home, I was barely able to lay down. I had difficulty breathing and clearing my lungs when horizontal, so I spent three nights in my wheelchair trying to cough up all of the mucus. Since I have no control of my diaphragm, coughing is extremely strenuous. I usually have to hook my right arm around the wheelchair's armrest and pull myself forward to force anything out of my windpipe. As a result of doing this for hours over multiple days, I ended up fracturing my right shoulder, my only working limb. This made it extremely difficult to drive my wheelchair, feed myself, or function at all, really. I haven't mentioned the negative effect on my pressure wounds from having to sit up for so long, but these were managed with the help of my wife, family and visiting nurses. I spent the next several weeks going back-and-forth to Massachusetts General Hospital for continued care of my wounds and shoulder.

Despite these unexpected health issues, I was beginning a new venture the following month and was very excited. I had been hired as the director of a summer program for teenagers living with a spinal cord injury (SCI) through BACKBONES, a non-profit that connects and supports people with SCI across the United States.[1] The program was designed to provide information and connections to help teens navigate obstacles they would encounter as they moved into adulthood. While preparing for the program, I reached out to other spinal cord communities. People liked the idea and its mission, saying there was no other program like it for the adolescent population. Sessions ran for two hours every Wednesday throughout the summer, and I got to know a great group of kids.

My time with these young adults went a long way in helping me cope this summer. This will become a theme throughout my narrative, but spending time with small children or teens, whether they are in a chair or on two feet, has always been an energetic, motivat-

---

[1]   To learn more about BACKBONES, visit BACKBONESONLINE.com.

ing experience for me, especially when needing an attitude adjustment. Taking in the perspective of somebody just starting out in life reminds us what is important and can propel us through low points or obstacles that seem daunting. Through the lens of each participant, I recognized myself more than 30 years ago. So much of the future is unknown at that age, and when a significant disability is added, apprehension and fear increase exponentially.

The program's message was not to sugar coat life, as they needed to understand their existence would be different and challenging. Even still, all of their dreams and desires were achievable; a full life was still a possibility. Each interaction was the perfect distraction for me at a time when I spent most of my day tilted back in my chair to relieve pressure on my backside. A few of the weeks, I was actually in bed during our Zoom calls. My predicament was an ideal illustration of how important it is for anyone living with SCI to care for their skin, especially on their bottom.

Not fully understanding the seriousness of my situation, we stopped in Long Island to visit grandchildren on our way home. Arlene's oldest son, Santino, is a firefighter and paramedic, and his girlfriend, Desiree, is a registered nurse, so we were confident we'd have medical assistance if necessary while we were there. Whenever I stay at another person's home, finding an accessible place to sleep is a challenge. The only option in Long Island was the bedroom of my five-year-old granddaughter. Gigi graciously allowed me to use her bedroom, while she got to have a sleepover upstairs with her two older brothers, Anthony and Domenic. I spent a week in a room with pink curtains, a pink bedspread and a Malibu Barbie dreamhouse. Each morning, Gigi joined me to play with Barbie and her younger sisters, Skipper, Stacy and Chelsea. How many 53-year-old, adult males know Barbie has 3 little sisters? Some mornings, seven-year-old Domenic was up early, so we had time together too.

The two children have always been inquisitive about how my body works. I have had to describe, for example, just how a super pubic tube goes into my belly so that I can pee in a bag. They often declare, "Michael, you're peeing!" when they see urine draining through the tube. Now that I have a colostomy bag, their level of curiosity has heightened even more. While we were discussing this one morning, Domenic turned to me with a straight face and said, "Wow, Michael, you're so lucky you get to pee and poop in bed anytime you want!" What an illuminating perspective on the inner workings of my body. His comment brought an instant smile to my face. Here was another example of the effect children have on me. Their honest, unabashed views on life almost always bring me out of a funk, and this was most definitely a time I needed something to help me smile.

When we finally arrived home at the end of August, a wound-care nurse came to assess my body and immediately sent me to the hospital. My sores had become severely infected. She was shocked that my body had not gone septic. Over the following two weeks, I had a couple surgeries to repair two of the infected areas. My third surgery was scheduled when we got word of the hurricane coming at Fort Myers. My first thoughts went to my wife, who would be alone in the house with me helpless to do anything, let alone be together. We were hoping that Arlene could stay at the hospital during the storm, but we learned she could not with the storm only hours away. With that news, we both lost our composure. Arlene had been home alone for days while I was recuperating in the hospital. Now she had to leave alone during the scariest hurricane we would ever encounter, and I'm her husband who's supposed to care for and protect her. I could no longer hold back my frustration and emotions—I don't think I've ever hated my life more than I did at that moment.

Arlene ended up staying with an old hockey friend from my hometown in Massachusetts. Craig and Charlene also live in Fort Myers, and I knew Arlene would be safe and comfortable. As I write now, the hurricane has added a terrifying layer to my situation, and my spirits are as low as I can ever remember. My own mortality is once again at the forefront of my mind. Is this worth it? What kind of life is this for my wife? Wouldn't it be easier for everybody if I wasn't here anymore? I want to be able to function. I want to be able to spend more time with Arlene. These are the fears I contemplate the entire time the wind picks up outside my window. My motivation is starting to wane; you never get a day off from being a quadriplegic. I am as tired mentally as I am physically. Part of me knows that, when my time here is done, there will be a small sigh of relief, my pain and stress will be over, and I can rest...but I'm afraid.

I've been living this way for more than 35 years, and I have enjoyed my life without regrets. The difference now is that it's not just me. There's another life involved; my existence affects my wife's. I can't get off the concept that I am failing Arlene. I am failing in my responsibility to be there for her in whatever capacity she needs and make her happy. Family and friends have told me how strong I am, but I don't feel strong at the moment. I have admitted aloud recently that this isn't as fun as it used to be. From a health perspective, my life is harder now than it has ever been. Having seen my share of downtimes, I have always picked myself up. Now, for the first time, I am having doubts. The "want to" just doesn't seem to be there right now. I think of Arlene, and she is where I find the fight, because I cannot fail her. I love my wife. I miss my wife.

Thursday, September 29, 2022

With Hurricane Ian in mind, I would amend my opening statement to, "No rolling forward, just rolling back, downhill, gaining speed." Now Ian has blown by, and my third surgery is indefinitely postponed. When the surgery was scheduled, a smooth recovery would have had me home in about 10 days. Instead, Fort Myers is in ruins, and the hospital is in lockdown. The city's water system was breached, and the hospital may have to be evacuated. This is one of four hospitals in the area suffering the same fate, so I may be moved to northern Florida, even further away from Arlene. Life just keeps knocking me backwards.

Though I struggle internally whenever I speak with her, I put up a front of positivity as I sense Arlene starting to break down. "I miss you, Michael. I want to be with you." She's crying on the phone, and I do my best to assure her that everything will be okay and that we will be together again soon. This does little to console her. She is still sobbing when she says, "Michael, nothing can happen to you.

We have just started together." She says, "You can't leave me now. There's so much more for us to do."

These words kickstart something inside of me. Though I'm rolling backwards fast metaphorically, I know Arlene is exactly right. I have to find my way back. There is so much more for us to experience together! Our phones get disconnected mid-conversation—cell service is scattered in the devastation—but her words are the spark that I'm looking for. As I lay crying in my bed, alone, not knowing when we will be together again, I type the following message: "I am surrounded by darkness and miss you so much. I hold on to hope knowing that, when the sun rises tomorrow and each morning after, I will be one day closer to holding you in my arms again!" The statement brings me solace, and motivation. I will not let this be my last chapter!

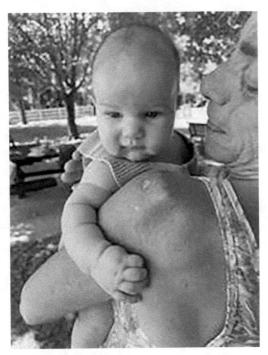

Summer, 2022. Proud grandma holding
newborn Genaro for the first time.

CHAPTER 2

"You'll Never Walk Again"

Friday, January 16, 1987

I scored the first goal of the game and was elated! My high school hockey team was on its way to its tenth straight victory—we were one of the favorites to win a state championship. The Zamboni cleaned the ice, and the buzzer went off for the second period. About halfway through the game, I skated into the corner with a player from the opposing team. As we went for the puck, my foot got caught and instead of skating left, momentum carried me straight. I hit my head on the board and felt a sharp pain in my neck. My legs crumpled underneath me as I fell backward on the ice. I landed on my back, with my left arm by my side and my right arm awkwardly above my head. I lay on the ice catching my breath for what felt like forever. The arena, once filled with the noise of fans and cheerleaders, was now silent. I couldn't pull my arm down for some reason, so I took another breath. When I went to get up, nothing happened.

Before my accident, I don't think I could even spell the word "quadriplegic," let alone imagine being one. That January night, during my senior year of high school, the doctors told me that I broke the vertebra at C5. As a result, I had lost all feeling and function below my chest and would spend the rest of my life confined to a wheelchair. Living as a quadriplegic means a life of unknowns. Most of my body functions independently from my mind, so an internal problem can put me in the emergency room without warning. I am incapable of moving, much less getting out of bed myself. I don't obsess over the myriad implications involved, but they always lurk in the back of my head. Life during COVID-19 has been similar to living with a spinal cord injury, wondering if you're feeling symptoms, lacking control over your own existence, and stressed by fear and uncertainty. Many have been forced to consider their own mortality. As a quadriplegic (aka "quad"), I think about these things every day of my life, yet I've come to value the opportunities I've gained from being in a wheelchair over what was taken away.

In the early days after my accident, I often heard, "things happen in life for a reason" or "it is all a part of God's plan." The truth is, what happened to me is not part of any plan; it is just a tragic aspect of life. "Why" will never be answered, and it is irrelevant anyway. Knowing why wouldn't change the fact that I'm sitting in a wheelchair. God's plan is what we do to find our way through adversity. When I focused on fixing one thing in my life (not everything at once), I was able to move on to the next. One simple change—one simple choice, no matter how seemingly insignificant—can impact the direction of your life. My first achievement was building enough strength to lift my arm onto a table. During my thirty-five years in a chair, I got a bachelor's of science degree in Education and dove into a job that was much more than a paycheck for me. I am honored to have made a difference in the lives of many adolescents and to have found the one thing that I longed for most, somebody to fill my heart.

My life illustrates that, as long as you control what is going on inside, you'll be able to handle anything life puts in front of you. To best understand how I got here, it's important to know who I was heading into that hockey game. Lessons I learned growing up laid an important foundation for dealing with the challenges I faced after my injury. Forgive the cliché, but the accident couldn't have happened at a worse time (to say the least). I was an honors student and had just turned eighteen.

It was a milestone I had looked forward to all of my life. Yes, sixteen meant that I got to drive a car, and twenty-one would mean that I could drink alcohol, but there was something different about turning eighteen. In the eyes of the law and my own, it was the birthday that gave me control over my life. I don't think I could have been more excited about my future. My first taste of independence would come at the end of each school day when I had "Student Union." Seniors who were over the age of eighteen could dismiss themselves for that last block. I had been looking forward to this privilege from the first day of school. In reality, it didn't mean much—it was about forty minutes before everybody else was released, and I usually had to be back at the end of school for some activity—but it was liberating and now mine to enjoy.

That Friday night, my family was celebrating my birthday. I was wearing my New England Patriots shirt with red three-quarter length sleeves that went down below my elbow. Those sleeves served two purposes: they looked good on the shirt, and they covered my skinny arms. I was not very proud of my body as a teenager. Wearing sleeves long enough to cover up was a great way to hide it, at least that's what my adolescent mind thought. My aunt and uncle joined us for a baked stuffed lobster dinner. I can feel the joy in my smile from a photo taken that night of me with my arm around my sister. It's the last one of me standing.

This was the beginning of a great weekend for me. The next morning, my undefeated hockey team had a game at eleven thirty. After the game, I'd be getting ready for a Saturday night date with my girlfriend. We were celebrating our three-year anniversary. I had made reservations at a nice restaurant and ordered flowers that I would pick up on my way home from the game. It was about 9 p.m. when everybody left after my birthday dinner. Our hockey team had a curfew the night before games, so I was not going anywhere. I decided to take a bath, one of my guilty pleasures growing up, where life just stopped, and my mind and body could relax.

The only bathtub in the house was in the guest bathroom. I was generally not allowed to use the guest bathroom, because my mother wanted to keep it neat for whenever company might be coming. I had to promise to "leave it exactly as I found it." I would bring in the mini-television that I'd won in a raffle from a road race my cross-country team ran earlier that year. I could sometimes even do my homework. I would sit in the bubble bath for over an hour and relish my time there. Only when I noticed I was getting pruney hands would I get out. I then primped and shaved, which at that point in my life didn't take very long—there wasn't much to actually shave. It was after 10:30 when I got into bed for a good night's sleep before my game. I remember a feeling of relaxation and comfort as my head hit the pillow. I was young and happy and excited about the future.

The next morning, I was on the road by 8:00 a.m. I drove to pick up one of my teammates, and we headed for the high school. We didn't talk much on the ride; we just turned up the volume on the radio. It was our usual routine on the way to a game, listening to an AC/DC cassette tape to get us motivated. From there, we got on the team bus and headed to the game. This season was going to be the fulfillment of a childhood dream. Our team was one of the best in the area, and we had a good chance of reaching the state finals. Going to the finals had been a hope of mine since I went as a little kid to watch my cousin play at the Boston Garden.

We had the first game of the day at Salem State and reached the arena early, so it was empty when we arrived. We mulled around outside the locker room. One of the players from the other team had played on a summer team with a group of us, so we talked with him a bit before it was time to get changed in the locker room. As I was getting dressed, I listened through headphones to my Walkman (a device that played music before iPods were around). I kept searching the radio for my lucky song by Billy Vera & the Beaters, called "At This Moment." It had become a ritual to hear it before every game. I went to Kiss 108, 94.5, 106.7, up and down each radio station, and couldn't find it. I didn't get to hear the song that particular morning, which I noticed but also knew wasn't really a big deal. I was confident that we were still going to win, as we were much better than the team we were playing.

In the first period, I was pumped after I scored the first goal of the game. It was halfway into the second period when I skated into the corner and hit my head on the boards. Our goalie was the first one over, saying, "Are you all right, Ruz?" The trainers hurried to me

across the ice. Everybody stopped skating and crowded arour.
The arena was so quiet. I never imagined that would be the last
I would ever be on skates, or for that matter, the last time on .
feet. My team would win the game and go on to play in the Bosto.
Garden later that year, which I would attend in a wheelchair.

After a while on my back, a trainer told me that my dad was
being escorted onto the ice. That's when I realized it must be really
bad. My dad was coming to me rather than staying in his usual spot.
I started skating as soon as I could walk. I have photos from my
childhood wearing double runner ice blades, leaning on a plastic
milk crate for balance. My dad played hockey when he was younger,
later coached, and now he was a referee. In fact, all of my relatives
played and coached at some point in their lives. My dad attended
every game I ever played—not as a coach, but as a spectator. I could
look at the same spot every game, and there he would be, on the glass
in the corner behind the net—he was never in the stands. (If you
know anything about hockey parents, then you understand why.)
Every game, wherever I played, he stood in that same spot.

I knew my dad was always proud of me, but he was frugal with
his praise. After games, my mother would say how wonderfully I'd
played. I was completely aware of the fact that she knew nothing
about hockey but was full of joy watching my number skate around
the ice. My dad's response to my performance was different than hers.
We would go over everything that I could do better next time—I
believe he felt the ride home after a game was the perfect time to
teach me. After games when he told me I played well, the ride home
would be quiet, but his silence spoke volumes to me. I would sit
back and relax with a contented smile on my face, knowing that he
was proud of me. I was blessed with the most loving and supportive
parents. When I'd see my father standing in that spot during games, I
knew everything was okay no matter what was happening on the ice.

That January day, when he walked onto the ice, I noticed my
father's eyes were glassy, and he looked at me in a manner I have
never seen before. There was fear in his eyes. It was the look a parent
has when they know their child is in trouble, and there's nothing
they can do to fix it. It felt like life paused for an instant, and I

.d that, when it restarted, life would never be the same again.

.ything that followed was a flurry. I was lifted onto a stretcher
 d wheeled off the ice. The arena went from silence to encouraging
 .pplause. I remember wanting to give a thumbs-up in appreciation,
but I couldn't.

Confusion and fear far outweighed any pain that I was feeling at that moment. I was placed in an ambulance and taken to the
emergency room of a local hospital. When they realized the severity
of my injury, I was transported to an emergency room in Boston.
At the hospital, the doctors stuck metal spikes into the side of my
skull, securing it to the bed to make sure my neck did not move.
After hours of testing—time that was excruciating—my family and a
couple doctors gathered around me. Each one of them looked at me
exactly the way my dad had earlier on the ice. Of course, one of the
doctors had to speak: "Michael, you have broken your neck. You will
never walk again."

That was it. Just like that. The life that I had known was over.
Hearing the words made me sick to my stomach, and I felt a pain in
my chest. Tears fell uncontrollably. Everyone kept telling me to relax,
trying to keep me calm. It wasn't necessary—I was numb. The rest
of that day was filled with additional testing and a constant flow of
doctors and nurses checking and repositioning me. I barely remember being transported to the fifth floor, a special wing of the hospital
designed specifically for SCI patients.

When my family left for the evening, a group of nurses came
into the room. They carefully propped me on my side using pillows,
a routine that would become familiar through the rest of my life.
They described each movement and explained why they were doing
it. If the nurses hadn't explained that they were moving my legs, I
wouldn't have known. The spikes fixed my head so that I could only
look straight. I was facing the window as they turned out the light
and left the room. I was alone for the first time that day. I stared out
the window, and reality set in. No matter how hard I tried, I could
not move any part of my body. Not only had I lost control of my
body, I realized I had lost control of my future. For the first time in
my life, I felt true heartbreak. Before I fell asleep that night, I stared

at the stars, and the last thought swimming around in my head was *I will never be able to reach for them again.*

There is no moment in my life that has influenced me more than that first night in the hospital. That night, I realized the fate of my existence was no longer in my control. It is a helpless, terrifying feeling. It's fear felt deep in your heart that you share with no other human being, and I relive the unsettling experience every night when my head hits the pillow. For just an instant, the realization that I cannot move from this spot without the help of another person sends little pangs of anxiety through my body.

Despite the radical change that my body has been through, the greatest change in my life has had nothing to do with my flesh and bones. The manner in which I would come to view every aspect of the world, and my place in it, was brand-new back then. As I've mentioned, I was afraid that not having control of my body meant that I'd also lose control of my life. Ironically, living life with SCI has enlightened me—experiences encompassing every aspect of my emotional pendulum have proven that having control of my body has little to do with controlling my life.

January 1987. Front page of the local newspaper—a tragic, life-changing moment. Thankfully, I had many more positive moments to follow.

CHAPTER 3

Learning to Live Life Again

Lying in bed before the first surgery of my life, my thoughts were immediate and functional. I didn't even know there was a body still attached to me. I couldn't feel it. I couldn't move it. At that point, I couldn't even raise my head to see it. The surgeons told me I had to wait for swelling to go down in my spinal cord so that they could fuse my fourth, fifth, and sixth vertebrae together. For two weeks, I lay in a hospital bed, getting turned by nurses every two hours to prevent pressure sores. These bed sores can happen if you lay on one spot of your body for too long. They actually develop from the inside of the body out, and you don't know they are there until it is too late. A pressure sore can develop in a few hours, though the recovery can last for weeks (as you saw in my opening chapter). This was the first of many new things I had to learn for life moving forward.

My skull was secured to the bed with spikes, as I mentioned, and a ten-pound weight hanging over the headboard. It was impossible for me to move my head in any direction, which was necessary to prevent any further damage to my spinal cord. I couldn't actually see what was going on overhead or below me. I really wouldn't know if something happened to my lower body.

At that point in recovery, there was no way possible to grasp the true reality of my new existence. Mentally, I didn't feel different yet—I was still an eighteen-year-old hockey player. I didn't quite process the true finality of the doctor's statement, "You will never walk again." Beyond the initial shock of hearing the words, what that actually meant for the rest of my life was not something that I was able to rationalize in the moment. One of the first things I heard from those closest to me was, "Michael, they are working on a cure for paralysis. It could happen any time." Yes, this was to give me comfort and hope in a situation that many deemed as hopeless. It was my first of many experiences where family and friends felt they had to protect me from my reality. They must have thought that repeating "never walk again" would be devastating to me.

As a show of positivity, I told myself and anybody around me that I would work as hard as I could. I convinced myself it was just an injury, and I would be up and around and back to normal someday. I even joked with my teammates that, when I got better, we would have to replay one of the hockey games I was going to miss. I am sure a lot of my ignorance was the result of shock. Is any human being equipped to fully comprehend such a dramatic and instant change in such a short amount of time? Rational thinking would have possibly had a negative consequence. Being naive about my new reality gave me hope at a time of devastation. There was going to be plenty of time later for rationally facing my new reality.

In the time after my surgery, there was a constant flow of visitors in and out of my room. My mother's sisters, Auntie Barbara and Auntie Gerry, were outside talking to anyone who came to visit, making sure visitors were positive and smiling when they came in to see me. They didn't want me to feel any worse or to see anybody feeling bad for me. Everybody walked in with a huge smile on their face and did everything they could to steer the conversation to something cheery. I don't remember much about what people said to me, but I do remember one thing vividly: the uneasy look in the eyes of every person that walked in. The people closest to me looked at me like I was not *me* anymore. Relationships that were as comfortable as could be were now awkward and anything but normal.

I was uncomfortable with each encounter, seeing and feeling the sympathy and apprehension in the people coming to see me. I made a conscious effort to put people at ease, to make the visit less awkward. Internally, my emotions were all over the place. I was most definitely heartbroken at that point. I was terrified of what lay ahead. Despite this, I made sure to express optimism for my future. I was motivated to make people see me as the same person. I, of course, had moments of devastation and despair. Even today, when I say that I broke my neck, it's *never* not a big deal, but life goes on. It was terrifying back then, and I was just being introduced to its magnitude. Throughout my life, I've come to realize there will be worry and curiosity when someone encounters me in a chair. The difference now is that I am fully aware of my reality, and I inherently engage to alleviate any unease that others feel around me.

As I said, I was on a floor designed for SCI patients. Who could imagine that an entire hospital floor was designed for spinal cord injuries? There were four patients in my room, with our beds separated by curtains and mine closest to the window. I was able to personalize my area, so memorabilia was scattered around the room—hockey sticks, cards, flowers, etc. On my ceiling was taped a huge card signed by just about everybody from my high school, along with family and friends. On nights that I'd lay on my back, I could take in all of the messages.

My view in the opposite direction of the window was a curtain that separated me from my nearest roommate, Paul. He arrived at the hospital several weeks before me. He'd had way too much to drink at a Bruins game, so his girlfriend kicked him out of the car. Walking home, Paul crossed an on-ramp and was hit by a car. He went through the windshield, which severed both his legs above the knee. He broke his second vertebrae and was put on a ventilator for the rest of his life.

For my first two weeks in the hospital, I wasn't able to get a good look at Paul. He was just a lot of beeps and blips from the machine that was keeping him alive. We spent the next four months as roommates, so you can imagine how I built a very close relationship with Paul there in the hospital. We shared the better part of twenty-four hours together, every day. At any point when I felt bad for myself or my situation, one look at what Paul was going through tempered those feelings.

Becoming a quadriplegic happened in an instant, but learning how to live as a quad took some time. Our day would begin every morning at seven with a change in the nursing shift. A primary nurse was assigned to two of the patients each day, and ours was named Kim. The morning started when Kim would remove the pillows around me, slide me from one side of the bed to the other, and turn me on the opposite side propped up by a pillow. The next hour was spent evacuating my bowel then getting catheterized to urinate.

Imagine. These are probably the most private aspects of a person's life, and here I was in a room with three other patients and nurses and other staff coming in and out. I literally had an audience! This was not an easy hurdle to overcome. In time, I realized it was a blessing to be on a floor with other spinal cord patients. I had to completely reshape my outlook on every aspect of life—physical and emotional—from what it was before my injury.

My roommates and I would next get a sponge bath, and our legs would be stretched for range of motion, to keep the blood flowing through our joints. We'd get dressed, which involved being rolled side to side in order to slide on a pair of sweatpants and a practically brand-new pair of sneakers—I noticed early that I would definitely get my money's worth out of sneakers. We basically lay around in our room every morning for two hours while other people tended to our needs. After the initial shock of learning how my body was going to function moving forward, the routine eventually felt natural, or as natural as possible post-injury.

Despite the various smells and sounds, that morning routine had a lively atmosphere—we would pass the time watching TV or listening to music. We were in close enough proximity that everybody in the room was involved. Kim had to be a translator because Paul could speak only in a whisper, given his tracheotomy and breathing tube. His laugh was something different. Paul's chest would heave up and down, and he could make a noise that resembled laughter. We would watch *$25,000 Pyramid* or some other game show, and I'd add color commentary to enhance our viewing pleasure. My intent was to make Paul laugh. Surprisingly, we were able to make light of our circumstances. Humor was important to distract us from our reality and the prospect of what life had in store for us.

The first time I got a good look at Paul was two days after my surgery to fuse vertebrae, about three weeks into my stay at the hospital. I was transferred into a wheelchair for the first time. My mother and father were there to witness the small but meaningful milestone in my recovery. My legs were wrapped tightly with Ace bandages to control the blood flow rushing from head to toe when I sat up. There were two nurses, one positioned in front of me and the other helping me get out of bed. I was raised to a seated position with both of my legs hanging off the side of the bed. Kim held my shoulders up, and the other nurse held me by the hips and slid me across what was called a slide board into a wheelchair. That first time sitting up, I felt the blood rush from my head, and my eyes instantly rolled back. The last thing I remember was my mother yelling to my dad, "Robert, Robert, what's happening to him?!" My mother almost passed out as well.

After I recovered, the wheelchair, which had been reclined, was slowly raised until I was in a seated position. Now with a clear view of my surroundings, I got to see Paul and all of the machines that were keeping him alive. He lay on his back with a sheet covering him up to his chest. His arms were positioned by his side on top of the sheet. When I looked at the bottom half of the bed, the sheet laid flat where his legs were supposed to be. It was startling and made me realize how much worse off he was than me. Still, whether he was in bed or in his wheelchair, Paul was always positive. We truly enjoyed the experiences we had together in the hospital. Seeing Paul smile and engage each day inspired me to want the same for myself.

On my initial wheeled trip down the hallway, I got a sense for the hospital environment. There were three sets of rooms on each side of the hallway and four patients in each room. My room was the farthest down on the right side of the hall. Only weeks prior, I'd been walking with not the slightest clue about life in a wheelchair. Now I was surprised at how many others were suffering the same fate.

We traveled down the hall, past the nurses' desk. We took a right-hand turn and passed the elevators and a family room for visitors before reaching the therapy room at the end of the hall. The therapy room had workshop tables on one side where we would receive occupational therapy. OT was my time to re-learn simple things—whatever I could physically attempt—like feeding myself and brushing my teeth. The opposite side of the room was dedicated to physical therapy. There were two mats against the back wall where I would be transferred to practice balancing so that I could safely sit alone. The first time I tried, I was suspended for a moment and then my body fell helplessly backward.

This balancing exercise became a daily ritual. The only parts of my body that I can control are my shoulders and my head, so I'd move my head and shoulders in one direction in order to offset the rest of my body moving the opposite direction. I gradually built up strength in my arms and shoulders to help with balance and got to the point where I could sit up for over a minute. I must have looked like a bobblehead when adjusting back and forth to maintain my balance. Ultimately, fatigue would set in and I would let myself fall backward. I couldn't move around much in my chair once I was positioned, and I wasn't able to move at all while in bed, but sitting on these mats helped me build strength and balance. Selfishly, I looked at it as my little bit of freedom, controlling my own body even for just a few seconds. It was the only thing I could physically do without help.

The therapy room was designed for all possible levels of spinal cord injury. There was a set of parallel bars on the side of the room where we did physical therapy. I'm sure most of you are familiar with parallel bars—their purpose at the hospital was to assist somebody having difficulty walking. Sitting in my chair, I viewed those bars much like I had a basketball rim before my injury. I could see the rim and want to dunk, but try as I may, there was no way that I could physically accomplish it. The parallel bars were an impossibility for me, but some spinal cord injuries are diagnosed as 'incomplete.' The spinal cord may only be partially damaged, making possible the restoration of function.

During my time at the hospital, only one patient arrived with an incomplete SCI. I remember two things about that patient's time in the hospital. The first was less significant than the other but equally memorable: he had sensation, so he could feel whenever they put in a catheter tube to empty his bladder—I won't forget his reaction the first time a tube was inserted! The second memory was a conversation we shared toward the end of his stay. After a few weeks, his legs became strong enough to stand on, and soon he was taking steps. The therapy room was filled on the day that he made his first solo walk from one end of the handrails to the other, a distance of about ten feet. Everybody in the room cheered at the accomplishment.

Shortly before he was supposed to leave the hospital (albeit on crutches), he and I had a quiet conversation. He said apologetically, "I am walking out of here, and I feel a bit guilty, because none of you will be able to." It was completely the wrong way to look at it, and I told him so. Any person able to walk after a spinal cord injury means one less person having to live in a chair. That person has no reason to apologize. He was right, though. There was no way I was going to walk out of the hospital. I had been forced to reevaluate my goals. Before my injury, I measured achievements on a much larger scale; everything was about major goals I wanted to accomplish in life. After my injury, I lowered the bar significantly given obvious limitations. I felt a great sense of satisfaction and accomplishment just being able to hold myself up for thirty seconds, having taken a while to get to the point where I could even sit up. My perspective had changed completely.

Where you break your neck determines what parts of your body still work. Of course, anyone can see that my legs don't work. With a higher level injury like mine, I also lost most of the function in my arms and have no control of my hands and fingers. I wear a brace on both of my wrists to keep my hands from flopping around. Retraining my right arm to move back and forth was one of the first things I had to do in physical therapy. I started with a simple exercise. My right arm and wrist were strapped to what looked like a mini skateboard that rolled back and forth on the big wooden table. I remember how hard I had to concentrate just to get that arm to move. I would be gritting my teeth and *willing* it to move. Though progress was slow, I was determined to work on the strength in that arm and was finally able to move my arm back and forth within a few weeks. A few weeks! I felt such accomplishment. Before that day,

I could never have imagined feeling satisfaction from something so simple.

My perspective about living a quality life changed, as it had to, really. During my senior year, I had written goals in the yearbook under my picture: graduate from college, get a job as an engineer, and buy a cherry-red Mercedes. Of course, it never crossed my mind that those goals would be replaced with being able to pick up my left arm when it fell down by my side. My stay at the hospital was a crucial adjustment period. I was surrounded by people who could take care of all my needs, and as I've said, the majority of patients looked just like me. This gave most of my peers and me a level of comfort in our environment that allowed us to enjoy our interactions and experiences each day. If someone peed their pants, there really wasn't much embarrassment, because everybody in the room would at some point have the same issue. The spirit was jovial as we gained strength and learned new things.

I worked daily with my occupational therapist, Jill, and there were usually a couple other patients around the table working with another therapist. The room was lively with a lot of conversation going back and forth. Jill was about twenty-four years old and very beautiful. There were some normal 18-year-old thoughts in my head at the time, and I was always motivated for occupational therapy. One particular morning, we laughed harder than we've ever laughed. I was practicing how to brush my teeth with Jill's assistance.

On the table were two cups, one filled with water and the other one empty. The water was for me to rinse, while the empty one was for my spit. Jill positioned the toothbrush in a little clip and slid it into the leather brace that was fastened around my wrist and palm by three straps. I began brushing my teeth. The toothbrush would only move so far, so I had to learn to manipulate my head in different directions to get every tooth. Jill was sitting back watching me brush and reached for her coffee cup, which looked just like the others. As soon as it touched her lips, she spat it right back out. Turns out, she sipped from the spit cup that I'd been using after brushing! Jill was leading the way as we sat around the table laughing.

21

The environment on our floor gained from how the patients helped each other. More seasoned patients and staff actually served as mentors. When I first got injured, for example, a few patients visited me in bed. Those who had been there for a significant amount of time were a positive influence on new patients, which made the transition to an unfamiliar existence easier. Even patients' family members did their part to make the new families comfortable. No *one* person becomes a quadriplegic—it is a change in lifestyle for the entire family and support system. Families intermingled in the visiting room, sometimes separate from their own family. It was a place to lean on each other emotionally, and they did, comforting each other and sharing details of how to manage the life of a quadriplegic. As so many other medical communities are, the SCI community has always been one where people do what they can to help somebody else along the way. A lot more than crying and consoling, families celebrated birthdays or other special events together. I was touched when, on Valentine's Day, my family set up a candlelit dinner in my little section of the room for my girlfriend and me.

Family and friends were allowed to visit at around 3:30 p.m. The visitors' room was always crowded. Most patients would be in the hospital for several months, so we got to know everyone's entire family. It was in the visitors' room that I learned my roommate, Lou, was related to a local personality: the lady who announced the next number when a table was ready at the Hilltop Restaurant. At the time, Hilltop was a popular steakhouse in my hometown, Saugus, just north of Boston. With a giant, lighted cactus and a dozen cow statues out front, the restaurant was enormous and attracted hundreds of diners each night. Patrons would line up along a lengthy breezeway with windows facing busy Route One. If you've driven that Northshore stretch of highway, then you know the towering cactus has become a landmark. Needless to say, I never had to wait in line at the Hilltop again!

I came to understand very quickly that time by myself was a rare and precious commodity. There's not too much that I can do without assistance, so I was surrounded by people from the moment I opened my eyes to the time I closed them at the end of another day. I began to cherish those few moments in my day when I needed nothing and did not have to bother anybody to help me. I volunteered to be the last one put into bed each night and often parked in the therapy room, listening to the new radio that had been donated by a former patient.

Waiting for my turn to be put into bed was my alone time. I sat solo and listened to Kiss108. Back then, Kiss was one of the hottest radio stations. I would feel myself relax and try to forget that there was a four-wheeled metal object under me taking the place of my legs. I would gaze out the window and listen to music, and for a few moments, I would feel like myself. Around 9:00 p.m. like clockwork, the DJ would play a remake of the song, "Lean on Me," by Club Nouveau. In case you don't know it, the lyrics croon soulfully, "Lean on me, when you're not strong." I would sing out the words every night with tears streaming down my face. I could put on a brave face during the day, but I was unable to fully comprehend, let alone get a handle on, the emotions resulting from this life-changing event. Alone at night was when I let my emotions out. I spent a lot of time in that room crying my eyes out. The main thing going through my mind was inevitably *how? How* am I going to live like this? I felt helpless and useless. What purpose would my life have? My head was filled with doubts, and I was terrified of the turn my life had taken.

I wouldn't see it coming, but like a shot in the arm, I got a glimpse into how my life could have purpose just a few weeks later. A young girl of sixteen came in after a car accident. She had broken her back at a point low enough that she was paraplegic. She had control of her arms and some control of her back, but everything below the waist was the same as for me—practically not there anymore. She was the first and only female patient on the entire floor. I was sitting in the therapy room one night when a nurse asked if I would go speak with the frightened girl, Anna. I couldn't imagine dealing with all the shock and fear that comes with SCI while also being the only female patient on the floor. I didn't even hesitate. Anna and I had a lengthy conversation about everything *except* our situations. There were even one or two times that I got her to smile just a bit.

Over the next few weeks, I spent a lot of time with Anna, talking and trying to assure her that things would eventually be better. I wasn't sure of anything myself and never knew what to say to the poor girl, but I wanted to give her hope. We generally talked about things that most teenagers do, friends and family, school, boyfriends and girlfriends. We did get around to sharing what landed us each in the hospital. We cried together at times, about the reality that neither of us would achieve the perfect happy ending we'd envisioned for our lives. More plentiful were the moments where there were just two teenagers having a conversation, and those represented hope for the future. For Anna, I wanted to acknowledge there would be tears down the road but emphasize that there'd be moments of joy, that *that* was the hope to hold on to. I realized that making her laugh and hopefully feel a little better about her future made me feel good about myself too. I was still able to have a positive impact on another person's life. I could see it through Anna's smile—I gave her assurance. It was one of the first times that I really felt I could have a purpose living this way.

My time in the hospital was a necessary period of transition. In many ways, my injury felt like waking up on a different planet. The hospital was a small community focused on teaching me how to acclimate to this new world. The SCI Floor provided a great environment to begin to understand what it would take both physically and mentally to exist in the world as a quadriplegic. I was initially filled with confusion and anger and directed it at anything and everything, trying to understand how and why this happened. I learned that one of the most powerful catalysts to moving forward—especially through tragedy—is forgiveness. I realized this during those many nights I spent alone, laughing one minute and crying the next. I had categorized my emotions and surmised that I would need to figure out some things mentally if I wanted to exist physically.

This first mental hurdle was possibly the most impactful along my journey. Getting rid of anger started with forgiveness. I spent time forgiving myself, forgiving my circumstances, and forgiving God, none of them actually to blame, of course. Forgiveness is not just about the recipient. It is a significant part of self-care, helping your inner person move through disheartening circumstances and shifting your energy toward hope. What sense does it make when a child is born with cancer or lives life with a disability? How does someone forgive the person who just shot their child? How does anyone get to the point they can't live without drugs or alcohol? How am I supposed to live my life with a broken neck?

I can empathize with anyone overwhelmed by those types of thoughts. Of course, circumstances may be completely different—we can't compare childhood cancer with an addiction—but the mental battle is similar. Physical obstacles seem so much more daunting when there is also a mental battle to overcome emotions like fear, anger, disappointment, and resentment. There came a point where I realized how destructive such thoughts could be to finding a path forward. Time wasted trying to blame someone or something for my circumstances was just that: time wasted.

Forgiving myself and anyone or anything that I deemed a contributing factor allowed me the opportunity to find a life worth living after my tragedy. Forgiveness, of course, did not change my physical circumstances, but it allowed me some peace to focus on finding a way through my negative emotions and rebuilding myself. Had I not recognized the waste of energy, I may never have written these words to hopefully help another family find their way through hopelessness. Of course, I didn't understand the extent of this epiphany in the short time I was at the hospital, but my time on the SCI Floor was an important building block toward long-term healing. I had gained comfort with my existence and was motivated to take advantage of the opportunities life would still put in front of me. When I was released from the hospital, it had been five months of intensive therapy, and I was ready!

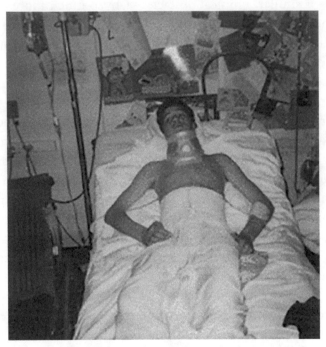

January 1987. My first few weeks in the hospital before surgery. I still have spikes immobilizing my head.

Chapter 4

Home Sweet Home?

I was finally going home. My chair was strapped in as we drove in a handicapped-accessible van over the Tobin Bridge. I was filled with feelings of both excitement and apprehension heading back home for the first time. When we got off the highway, yellow ribbons were tied around the trees lining the streets from the exit right up to my front door. We were unable to park in the driveway, as it was filled with family and friends who were there to welcome me home. The moment I got off the lift and rolled into the driveway, my two grandmothers ran over to give me a big hug and kiss. It was a great welcome home, as I hadn't seen my grandmothers while in the hospital. Being home with my family was a huge relief.

The appearance of my home had not changed, but now I looked at it altogether differently. The van's ramp could not deploy on our slanted driveway, so I had to be let out on the street. We lived in a split-level home, and the front steps that I walked up and down my whole life were no longer accessible. There was no automatic door and no elevator. I entered through the garage and up a small ramp into the basement, which had two small windows facing the bushes in front of the house. It was otherwise simple wood paneling on top of a concrete foundation. When I entered from the garage that first day, I saw a hospital bed where our black octagonal table once sat. The site of many poker games with my friends wasn't there anymore. Opposite the bed remained the portable bar that my parents had set

27

up years ago (most definitely not a place where my sister and I ever tried to sneak alcohol). Behind the bar was our boiler room, where I used to dry my hockey equipment. Finally, on the far side of the room was the den with stairs that led to the second floor.

The den was where I spent much of my childhood. Every part of that basement had special meaning for me. As a little kid, I sat on the stairs and peeked through the wrought-iron railing to watch the television in the corner. We had a black vinyl couch on the back wall, and there was a fireplace framed by two glass wine racks, each enclosed by a decorative wrought-iron door. The fireplace reminded me of playing knee hockey, using the fire screen as our net. (There were a few glass casualties during games over the years.) The couch was always my goal line. I used to move it to the middle of the room when I played football by myself. On the last play of my game, I would dive over the goal line for the game-winning touchdown. The basement was also the room where I had my first beer. It had essentially been my personal hangout. Now, it was my bedroom. The "good old" basement felt strange and new. I never realized how dark it got down there at night and how much noise the boiler made.

As much as I was relieved to be home, I realized that first week just how much the world was *not* built for someone like me. I was no longer comforted by the routine of the hospital, where people were trained to take care of me and did so when I needed it. No more waking up to game shows on the television in a room full of wheelchairs and spending my day learning to live again. The first morning I woke at home, two visiting nurses came to help me out of bed. They had trouble transferring me into my wheelchair and had to lower me down to the floor, having basically missed the chair. My family helped me get up, fortunately, and the nursing company sent two other people the next day. Every structure was an obstacle, and simple, everyday objects were out of my reach. Things had to be set up for me before I could do anything, even brush my teeth, get a drink of water, or watch TV. At home, I was like an alien on a new planet or Dorothy arriving in Oz—I wasn't "in Kansas anymore, Toto."

If I wanted to go outside, make a phone call, or do just about anything, it meant imposing on somebody else to help me. There was no such thing as voice technology in 1987, and the cell phone was still a decade away. Simple communication was a major obstacle for me, so personal relationships were hard to maintain. For a short time, I was able to keep in touch with friends from the hospital, but imagine the situation on both ends. It was like connecting through an interpreter since we couldn't dial the call or simply plan to meet somewhere. As time passed, unfortunately, the relationships I formed in the hospital became more and more difficult to maintain. With today's technology, I have gotten to know many people in the SCI community. It is always helpful communicating with people who live life from a similar perspective. Back in the '80s, it was a struggle.

I could immediately see how my homecoming would disrupt the lives of my family. My family set up a routine and schedule when I first got home. We needed to ensure that someone would be around throughout the day and night—I required similar care to what you would arrange for a newborn infant. The caregivers had to make sure that every detail of my life was understood, and someone had to be available at a moment's notice. My family went out of their way to make sure I had everything that I needed. I am so grateful and blessed to have a mother, father, and sister who sacrificed so much of their lives to accommodate mine. I learned to accept my limitations, because there was nothing I could do to change them, but realizing the burden my life was now going to be on everybody else's was very disconcerting.

Not being able to participate in so much of my own existence was difficult, so I started playing a mental game with myself soon after I moved back home. I mapped out the easiest possible route for every aspect of my day, knowing that I had to instruct another human being to do for me everything that most people do unconsciously. To get out of bed, take a shower, or get a drink of water, I learned my parents' schedules and chose the least inconvenient time to disrupt them. I tried to kill at least half a dozen birds with one stone when running errands on someone else's time. I ate not when I was hungry, but when it fit someone's availability. I learned to take large bites of a sandwich to minimize how often someone would need to lift it to my mouth. As time passed, I figured out how to weave all the needs of my life into the life of whomever I was with, to lessen the inconvenience. Now that mental game has become second nature.

In the hospital, I had learned how to function as a quadriplegic. The next question was, could I actually have fun sitting while everybody else was standing? I found the answer to that question on a dance floor. I have always felt that I had the soul of a dancer. Pre-injury, I was complimented more than once on my dancing ability. My parents were in their twenties during the disco era, so music and dancing were a large part of my childhood. I had at least a half-dozen family members who owned DJ companies that were hired for weddings, anniversaries, and graduations. This also meant that, whenever there was a family occasion, music would play an important role. I grew up listening to popular music and was not shy to express myself on the dance floor. I practiced my moves in front of the mirror, trying to perfect my moonwalk. In my head, my dancing ability was on par with Michael Jackson. Unfortunately, *America's Got Talent* was not around back then—I could have taken my life in a completely different direction.

After my injury, we still had family dance parties, but now I was sitting on the outside observing what was going on. I'd rationalize that my chair takes up too much space on the dance floor, that I'd probably bump into people, and someone would get hurt. More importantly, I worried I'd look like a freak—how do you dance if you don't have use of your legs? Excuses kept me from participating until I had a revelation as the result of what I witnessed.

There is something liberated in people when they are dancing. Much the way I practiced moves in front of a mirror, people let go of their inhibitions on the dance floor. They think they are Patrick Swayze or Jennifer Grey in the final scene of *Dirty Dancing*. The visuals on my side of the dance floor were very different—the dancer on the outside rarely reflected the dancer on the inside. I say it with love, but clearly, all that mattered to the people on the dance floor was the way that they felt inside. They weren't thinking about how they might look. Dance represented how they felt about themselves and the freedom to express it. I realized after a while that I couldn't look more ridiculous dancing than anybody else. Finding comfort on the dance floor after my injury was a big step for me. I know what I must look like when dancing, but now it doesn't matter. In my mind, I am still jumping up on my toes trying to perfect the moonwalk—in a wheelchair—so now it would be more like a moonride.

Today I still feel that I have the soul of a dancer. After getting our vaccinations, my wife and I recently went dancing with a new sense of freedom to get out and enjoy our lives again. I did something I haven't done in thirty years—we stayed at the nightclub until last call. My friends from college would be shocked. (In full disclosure, we live in Florida, so last call was at 9:45 p.m.) Florida has turned back into a spring break haven, only now, most of the spring breakers are retired and probably have replaced a body part. The radius of my chair allows me to have three or more dance partners at a time. The chair is like a magnet for women. It is a rare occasion when other men look at me and feel a bit of envy. I'm not sure if they are envious of me dancing with multiple women or because I am lucky enough to be able to sit down while I dance.

It is one thing to overcome uncertainty on the dance floor, but it was another story when feeling different extended through the rest of my life. When I first returned home, certain people, places, and things that had once been comfortable now seemed different. I remember wondering whether it was me who was different. I wasn't sure. In those first years at home, there would be many times that something I once found natural became a source of anxiety. My first solo experience outside the house was going to be attending college, about a year after my accident. I had been really excited about that next chapter of my life, but now, the prospect of going into the city every day for class at Boston University (BU) petrified me.

Growing up, the first day of school was always something that I looked forward to. My mother picked out my clothes when I was young. (Like most of us, I look back and ask my parents how they could ever have made me wear those clothes.) My mother would take a picture of my sister and me on the front steps in our first-day outfits. For eleven years, we repeated the same general routine, though in middle school, we moved to the other side of town, around the corner from my aunt. I traded in my Toughskins for Sergio Valente jeans, which I wore with Nike Cortez sneakers. School was a place of comfort for me, and I looked forward to the beginning of each year.

I began college at BU in January 1988. After my months at the hospital in Florida. The feelings I had leading up to my first day of college were eye-opening. I became increasingly apprehensive as the date approached. The reality was that I had to leave my comfort zone, again. I didn't know people there. How would I get someone to help me? How would I even get around? It was the first time that I experienced the world on my own from a wheelchair, and I had to get dropped off in downtown Boston. After sitting in traffic for an hour my first day, I drove by Fenway Park onto Commonwealth Avenue, where BU was located. There was not a lot of parking, so we had to pull into a lot and double park briefly to let me out of the van.

The sidewalks were filled with people walking in both directions. Getting from the parking lot to the sidewalk was not an easy task. I couldn't just blend in with everybody. I had to pause, much like a driver waiting to get on to a busy highway. I would look to my left and right at all of the traffic. People walked in both directions, so I needed enough time and space to weave in. I would inch closer until I eventually found my opening and drove on to the sidewalk. It was overwhelming, trying to pay attention to both the people in front of me and the obstacles beneath me, constantly looking up and down to navigate the sidewalk. Once I made my way to the end of the street, I realized that had been the easy part!

Next I had to cross Commonwealth Avenue. This was Boston traffic, with three lanes going in both directions and above-ground subway tracks in the median, also moving in both directions. The moment the "walk" light came on, masses of people began to move. I had to avoid the pedestrians passing in either direction, while automobiles stopped at the red light added stress. Halfway across, I looked down at the train tracks I'd dreaded. I had to drive over a dozen tracks to get from one side of the street to the other. Bump over one, bump down, bump over, bump down, bump over, bump down. When I finally made it over the tracks, I had three more car lanes to cross. I looked up at the streetlight and saw the countdown, nine…eight…seven…I had to get across! Which I did, just in time.

My reward was another sidewalk. It was thankfully narrow and less busy, so I could actually relax and enjoy my trip down the side street, where, at the end, I took a left turn to get to my first class.

I was traveling between two tall buildings on a back street of Boston, feeling the wind of that cold January afternoon, when I noticed someone in the distance. On the opposite side of the street was another man in a wheelchair driving toward me. He was about two hundred yards away, and I couldn't take my eyes off him. I stopped on the sidewalk and stared. I noticed the way that he hunched over in his chair. The strange way his arms moved. The placement of his feet on the footrest. And of course, the wheelchair in which he was sitting. How could I miss it? I focused on every detail that made him look different from everybody else. My eyes stayed fixed on him as he approached the building across the street, waited for someone to help him open the door, and disappeared.

At the time, I lamented internally, "That's me. *That's* how I look." Seeing that man solidified in my brain that I was deeply different. I didn't know it, but at that moment, I'd planted a seed that would impact the way I'd see myself for decades: it *was* me, not the world, that was different. In many ways, feeling different had as much of an impact on my life as did breaking my neck. Especially when I was in college, the feeling that everybody was looking at me made me self-conscious and doubtful. I would eat lunch in my van to avoid people. Periodically, I would venture to a Burger King on Commonwealth Avenue, where they had walls of glass, and I could feel the sun on a cloudless winter day without being outdoors. I also liked to people-watch. Hordes of people of various races, shapes and sizes moved in both directions. I watched short legs and long legs, the way they moved, and how people took one step, then another, without even thinking about it. I would look down at my own legs, willing them to just move. I would actually shake from trying to concentrate, but with the same result every time, of course. Nothing.

The anticipation of what could go wrong was always stressful. Something as simple as a lunch out could become a disaster pretty quickly. There was a girl from my high school who also went to BU. She lived on campus, and we planned to meet for lunch one afternoon. We had been in honors classes together during high school, so we spent most days in each other's company. I didn't understand why the prospect of having lunch with her created so much anxiety, until I imagined actually sitting down together. It would take five minutes to get positioned under a table, so I decided I'd get situated early. That was one hurdle. As for the actual lunch, it would be the first time I was with somebody that had no idea of my needs. She wouldn't know how to place my fork in the brace, and what if I needed to cut my food? I fumbled my way through getting my fork in my brace before she got there. I also looked at the menu and found something to eat that wouldn't require cutting (which left out sandwiches, for example).

It was ten minutes before my friend was to arrive—not a good thing for someone feeling anxious, so I started to bite at a nail. I was always a nervous nail-biter as a kid. I still had the habit after my injury, but now without feeling in any of my fingers. Biting my nails could quickly turn into a scene from a horror movie. That day, I was chewing the thumbnail on my right hand. No sooner did it start to bleed than my friend walked up to the table. While we said hello and picked out our order, I kept my hand under the table and tried to inconspicuously put pressure on my thumb, pushing it against my pant leg. The bleeding was on the same hand as my brace and fork, so I had to quickly take a bite of food and put my hand back underneath the table to avoid my friend noticing. My system worked. I survived the lunch. I let her leave first, which was smart, because when I backed out, my lap looked like a crime scene.

That lunch epitomized my time in college. I spent a lot of time alone and afraid, because I felt different, but I significantly matured into life in a wheelchair. As it was with most aspects of being a quadriplegic, I had to find a way to adapt both physically and mentally. I had no choice; my existence was not going to change.

2017. My parents. Mom and Dad, none of this would
have been possible without your love and support!

CHAPTER 5

More than Four Wheels

The first day I was transferred into my new motorized wheelchair, I looked at it as I would a new automobile. Everything was clean and shiny, and I couldn't wait to get in it. I was at the hospital about four weeks after my accident, and it was my inaugural "roll" back to some semblance of independence. I could actually move the wheelchair myself. The freedom made a huge difference for my psyche and my motivation.

There was an attachment on the wheelchair's joystick to help me drive, and I could adjust the speed with a lever that displayed a turtle for slow and a rabbit for fast. It took a while for me to build up the strength to become a skilled driver. I definitely needed turtle mode initially—driving a straight line was not easy—but it didn't take me long to get comfortable. I looked forward to each day once I was in that chair, around 9:00 a.m. I would exit through my room's wide doorway. The corridor was always filled with people and clutter scattered around—laundry baskets, computer tables, and food carts, among other things. As a new wheelchair driver, it was like an obstacle course to get from one end to the other. I'd weave my way past all of the patient rooms and the nurses' desk and take a right turn toward the therapy room. No longer would something be only an arm's length away from me but out of reach!

Even now when I wake up, I check for sunshine outside and my wheelchair in the corner of my bedroom. My day doesn't begin until I am comfortably in my chair. When I flick the On switch and push the joystick forward, I still feel a jolt of excitement, a sense of freedom and independence, like in those first weeks learning to drive. The process of getting into my chair was initially time-consuming and awkward, so it evolved over the years. In the hospital, transfer required a pair of nurses and a slide board, but at home, we quickly eliminated the board. For many years, I relied on people lifting me in and out of my chair. My friends and family were younger, and I was lighter at that point in my life. Over time, sitting in a wheelchair made putting on weight unavoidable. My outlook on weight and exercise was much like the character played by John Candy in the movie, *Stripes*, who described basic training as "perfect for what I need! My counselor told me I swallow a lot of aggression along with a lot of pizza." As a person who loves to eat, I could identify with the sentiment.

My personal care attendant, Jeff, was the only one who could lift me by himself, which made the morning process very easy. In less than thirty minutes, we could be in and out of the shower, back to my bed to get dressed, and into my chair. I say we, but I didn't do much more than flop around while he did all the work. That's been the story of my life, lying or sitting around while other people do my bidding! I say this in jest, but it really does describe my day-to-day existence. I was extremely lucky to have Jeff, who I've known since childhood, take care of me for more than twenty years.

One of the most challenging things to deal with after my injury was orchestrating bedtimes. I hardly ever had a choice in what time I could get out of bed or even when I'd get into bed for that matter. Since I needed assistance, daily transfer in and out of bed was one of the activities that took a lot of thought. I planned ahead for who might help, as it was a regular source of anxiety for me. I was fortunate to have a lot of relatives living nearby. Most of them understood the need and learned how to get me in and out of bed. A large group of family and friends were ready to help me at a moment's notice, but I still felt anxiety in having to bother them. I dreaded calling somebody close to me, knowing the first thing I would hear was, "What do you need?" How much my existence depends on others has taken a great emotional toll.

Now that I am married, I don't have to be on a schedule for the first time in my life. My eyes usually open around 5:00 a.m. I "OK Google" to send a text to Arlene, who is sitting out on our lanai, sipping her second cup of coffee by then. After lying on my side all night, I need her to come change my position. I hear the floor creak as Arlene steps on the ramp to come in from the lanai. She first takes a right turn to the Keurig to prepare cup number three. While that is brewing, she walks across the hall into our bedroom. Arlene's very efficient now—she pulls the wedge out from behind my back and empties the urine bag at the end of the bed. She takes the pillow out from between my knees, reaches her hands into slots in the pad underneath me, and pulls my body to the side so that I fall straight onto my back. Arlene repositions my legs and drainage bag, raises the head of the bed, and puts the TV clicker on the shelf in front of me (aka my belly).

Now comfortably on my back, the first thing I do is swing my left arm out to the side and luxuriate in all of the space. I love my wife very much, but if you ask me what was the most difficult thing to give up after being single for forty-five years, it would be having a bed to myself when I sleep. Arlene doesn't have the "Jimmy Legs" that Kramer had to deal with on *Seinfeld*, but I take up so much space that there's actually not much room for her. When I am able to have the bed to myself, I relish the comfort. Then again, sharing the bed is a small sacrifice when I get to wake up each morning looking into Arlene's beautiful blue eyes.

Depending on whether I shower, getting dressed takes anywhere from fifteen minutes to an hour and fifteen minutes. We actually have it down to a science. The bed is at the perfect height, so Arlene does not have to bend over to sponge-bathe me. From there, she rolls me onto my side and places a sling underneath me. Our system has evolved, so the only time Arlene ever has to roll me is to get me on and off that sling—we have almost perfected the zero-physical-exertion transfer.

Arlene wheels a large steel arm over to the bed, where the sling is attached. This apparatus is called a Hoyer Lift, and for me, it's one of the greatest inventions in the last quarter-century. With the press of a button, I am lifted into the air and float over the bed until Arlene swings me over my wheelchair and presses the button again. As the lift lowers me, Arlene pulls me in the sling so that my butt is at the back of the chair. Once settled, the sling's loops hooked around the lift loosen up. With relatively good strength in my right arm, I feverishly race to take off the loop near my right shoulder before Arlene gets done with the other three. I always point out when I beat her, though she responds, "Yeah, but I had to do three." I also figure I'm helping out a little bit.

We have adapted all of my clothing to make it easier for Arlene to get me dressed. I would usually be rolled from side to side while my clothing is gradually pulled to where it needs to be. To eliminate that step, we have cut out the back of all my shorts to become easy-on, easy-off clothing. Arlene tucks the excess material around my legs and butt. That is right, America, the only thing between you and my naked body is a strong breeze. From there, a shirt is pulled over my head and tucked around my belly, and I am dressed in less than two minutes. My mother designed holes in the sides of each shirt to accommodate the wheelchair's chest strap. The strap wraps around my chest, hidden under my shirt, to prevent me from falling forward out of my chair. At a glance, nobody would notice anything unusual about my attire.

As long as the chair remains upright, my life is pretty good. Yes, there have been mishaps when my wheelchair has tipped over. One of the more interesting occasions occurred in the presence of twelve kids under the age of ten and four women over the age of sixty-five. As a forty-something, I volunteered at my church in an after-school program, and we would go to the playground after homework was completed. That particular day, I decided to stop a basketball from rolling across the parking lot. I had done it a hundred times before, angling so the ball would hit me and stop rolling, but physics was not on my side that day. My wheel rolled perfectly up on the textured round basketball and lifted the right side of my wheelchair in the air, tipping me over.

My head and my body hit the ground, but I didn't really realize what had happened, until I saw the shocked faces of everybody looking down at me. As if the crash wasn't enough, my shorts were no longer covering me! Donna, one of the volunteers, a retired nurse, made sure that I was okay and got me a blanket. I laid there until the fire department came, righted my chair, and lifted me back into it. I was a bit disheveled but otherwise okay. When Arlene came a short time later, she must have said, "What happened?" four times before reaching me at the end of the hallway. Arlene kept checking my arms and legs as if concerned they weren't attached. I spent a few minutes calming her down, but we went to the emergency room, just in case, and spent eight hours on Valentine's Day waiting to get x-rayed. Everything did turn out fine, and actually, I still get Christmas cards from the four women that witnessed my little tumble. I must have made quite an impression. As for the little kids, they will have to explain about the man in the wheelchair coming out of his shorts to their therapists later in life!

Being in a wheelchair makes it difficult to express personal style. In the grand scheme of my existence, it may not seem like a big deal, but think about how much attention you pay to your own appearance before you leave the house. What is the clothing material like? Does it match, and will it be easy to put on? Will it keep me warm? Back in the hospital, I wasn't overly concerned with my appearance—sweatpants and a sweatshirt were my daily attire—but I quickly became aware after seeing myself in a picture from my senior prom in high school. I attended the prom after being released from the hospital in May 1987. I did not have a handicapped-accessible vehicle at the time, so I had to attend in my manual wheelchair and was unable to move without someone pushing me. My friends and their dates met at our house for pictures in my driveway. I sat in one spot for a half hour, facing directly into the sun. By the time the pictures were done and we headed to prom, I had a bright, rosy sunburn on my face.

My date and I were king and queen of the prom. (I'm sure I got a few sympathy votes for the wheelchair, but a win is a win!) A photo was taken of the two of us wearing our crown and tiara. In it, my face is bright red and the bottom of each pant leg ends about halfway down my calf. If you're old enough to understand what it means to have "floods" on, then you understand what I am describing. My family was learning how to live with and dress me just as I was, and there is a method to putting pants on a spinal cord patient. I could lie on a bed with pants looking perfectly normal, but when transferred into a chair and properly positioned, pants can ride up in the crotch area. That night at prom, my pants looked like the capri pants that Mary Tyler Moore wore in the 1960s.

Fortunately, I do not have to wear pants very often these days because the weather in Florida is always warm (*not* because my wife and I joined a nudist colony). I remain self-conscious and am very particular about the length of my shorts. If one side is shorter than the other, I push until it's even with the other side, just above my knees. I'm also very particular about how my feet are positioned on the foot rests. Even if one foot is slightly off to the side, it bothers me. When I can't fix it myself, I get sidetracked. I may try to look away and pay attention to something else, but my focus always returns to my crooked foot. It is like having an itch out of reach in the center of your back, so you try to ignore it, but you can't get it off your mind. I now drive to a pole or corner of a piece of furniture and carefully adjust them to the precise position I like, and then I feel relief.

I was always conscious of my appearance, and I never liked drawing attention to myself. I vividly remember my chair breaking the night before a friend's wedding, so I could no longer drive as one of the ushers. I had to be pushed and sulked the entire wedding, having made a spectacle when my intention was to hide in the background. This desire even influenced the color of my chair. I have always had a black wheelchair because I thought the color would be less noticeable. Black always seemed the best color to minimize attention. Every storage bag that I attached to my chair was black. I scraped off a yellow manufacturer's label since it made my chair stand out more. If I could have made the wheels black, I would have. The other benefit with black is common fashion knowledge: wearing black is slimming (though there's still no shade that would hide the bowling ball that is my belly)!

I've spent a lot of time considering how to camouflage it but have come to realize that I need to embrace my wheelchair. There is no getting around the fact that I need it to exist. I don't even think of myself as sitting in my wheelchair anymore. Only when I catch my reflection in a mirror or window am I reminded of what everybody else sees. My wheelchair is a part of me. I mean, you can't notice me without noticing my wheelchair—it'd be like walking next to Shaquille O'Neal and not noticing that he's tall. It took me some time to accept, but of course, having a wheelchair makes me no less of a person; it just means that I can't walk and need it to get around.

In 2020, I got a new wheelchair. I had no say in picking out my chair, as it was given to me by a family from my hometown. It is a bright and shiny blue, and I love it. The entire frame is blue, the foot rests are blue, and I was thinking about getting spinners on the tires. When I first got injured, I spent a lot of time around the corner at my cousin Stephen's house. Across the street lived a man, Huey, who was also quadriplegic. Huey and I spent a lot of time together at that point in our lives and maintained a connection for many years. As I've said, the spinal cord community is just that—a true community of not only people in wheelchairs, but their families and friends too. Everybody involved in our lives knows the sacrifices necessary to care for us. We all empathize with other families going through similar circumstances.

Huey passed away a few years ago. He had been married for two years and was very happy. Two weeks before passing, his new wheelchair had arrived at his house. He had a stroke the next day, which eventually took his life. Huey was only able to sit in the chair once for about fifteen minutes. Though he and I had not seen each other for years, I mourned both for Huey and the loss that his family must be feeling. The sad news of his passing triggered my own introspection. His death was a stark reminder of the fragile life of a spinal cord patient. I reflected on time—the time that Huey spent in this world, the time that he missed out on because he died so young, and the time he will have now, relieved of the pain and suffering that came with his existence. I love my life and in no way want my time to be over, but I understand there will be some relief, and Huey knew that as well as anyone. Time is a precious commodity, and no person is promised a future. Spending more than half my life in a wheelchair has helped me appreciate being present.

A short time after Huey passed away, his family reached out to ask if I would be interested in the wheelchair. I was overwhelmed by the suggestion. A wheelchair costs more than $30,000, and this grieving family was kind enough to offer the chair to me? It was the exact chair that I used, only brand-new, and of course, bright blue. After spending $10,000 to have it custom fit to my body, I received a very generous donation from the Travis Roy Foundation to help defray the cost. Travis was another hockey player injured a few years after me, only eleven seconds into his first shift at Boston University, ironically. Travis passed away in 2020, sadly, but much like Huey, his positive impact has improved the lives of so many.

The morning after the new chair arrived, I stared at it from bed in anticipation. I remember thinking, *People are definitely going to notice me now.* Huey's wheelchair has now been a part of many new experiences for me. Just prior to the pandemic, Arlene and I went on our first cruise. Along the way, we bought a new backpack for my wheelchair. It was a brightly colored, beautiful New England Patriots bag. I know that might make people angry or not like me, but I do not apologize! I grew up listening to my dad and uncles—all season ticket holders—complain about sitting on steel benches, freezing just to watch them lose...until they started winning around the turn of the century. Even though Tom Brady is wearing a different uniform, he is now only two hours away from me, so I have two teams to cheer for in the Super Bowl. That Pats bag will further adorn my new blue chair and remind me of our trip.

Whenever I've traveled, it's been in a group with lots of people to take care of me. I love my family and friends, and with them, I have spent many great times on vacation in my two favorite spots, Florida and Las Vegas. I cherish the memories we made. This vacation, however, was just my wife and me. It was wonderful for many reasons, most notably that we didn't have to fly anywhere. Fort Lauderdale was a two-hour drive, and my stepson, Pasquale, was generous enough to take us. Once we were aboard, everything we wanted was within rolling distance. It would be a true holiday without having to worry about transportation. As long as the boat didn't sink, it was perfect for me!

When we travel, Arlene and I are always nervous about our room's accessibility. On the ship, our state room was truly handicapped-accessible. There was an accessible shower, and our lift fit easily under the bed. Unlike most hotel rooms, there was plenty of space to maneuver. We even had a huge balcony that I could enjoy. The room was perfect. Each morning, we had breakfast delivered to our room and ate out on the balcony. It was exquisite just watching the waves, the vast, serene ocean and other cruise ships passing by. We would later spend time by the pool or wander around the boat. Afternoons were back on our balcony to relax. A few times, we were in the middle of the Atlantic Ocean, with no land as far as the eye could see, and we'd see a bird flying about the ship. I found it amazing that a bird could be casually flying by that far away from land—talk about having control of your life.

We always went to the dining room for dinner, where we had our own table right at the entrance. It was a five-star three-course dinner every night. The staff was so attentive and friendly that anything we needed was there at a moment's notice. We had one noteworthy mishap when a gentleman driving his scooter saw a space between our table and the wall. I happened to notice he was wearing sunglasses and had a walking stick on the scooter. He thought he could squeeze through but miscalculated when he passed our table. I looked up from my lobster tail to see my wife, with her knife and fork in hand, being dragged away from the table. Three or four wait staff went running—the driver had no idea that Arlene was attached!

Being able to go on a vacation alone with my wife had deep, personal meaning to both of us. This was my first vacation without a specific caregiver—Arlene and I were contentedly on our own. One of the best aspects of marrying Arlene is that so many of the things we do are firsts for both of us. It makes the experience all the more special for me, and this cruise was no exception. The Pats bag on my chair is a reminder of that wonderful cruise and the day we shopped in Cozumel, Mexico. The colorful bag is also symbolic of my own evolution.

I used to be apprehensive about standing out in a crowd, as I've said, but I no longer mind being different. In fact, I think about my wheelchair these days about as often as someone would think about their feet. Unless you step on something or have an issue, you wake up every day not thinking about your feet. Meanwhile, they support every single step you take throughout the day. The same with my wheelchair. I am not aware of it unless there is an issue. I get in my chair much like anybody else puts on a pair of shoes. I am not trying to minimize my life—a piece of my heart will always be broken as a result of that day. My existence is different than I ever imagined it would be—different from just about everybody else in the world—but that's okay with me now.

This is my time. I want people to notice my wheelchair. I want people to see that I am different. I want people to look at me living life with a smile on my face and say, "I can do that too." It is my wheelchair that makes me different, and if my life is an example of anything, it demonstrates that there is a place for difference in this world.

Spring, 2018. Docking in Cozumel, Mexico. Best vacation ever!

CHAPTER 6

Finding My Purpose

Sitting in my first wheelchair gave me a great sense of independence once I left the hospital. It also gave me a whole new set of fears. I could drive the chair around, but now I had to find a destination. What could I do to be a contributing human being while sitting in a wheelchair? That was my overwhelming concern when I was in college. Choosing a direction in life at the age of eighteen is hard enough on two feet. It seemed there wasn't much I could do for a living, the obvious disqualifying me from many professions. Sure, I was going to college, but why? Having to start somewhere, I began as a Communications major but changed it soon after learning how much reading and writing was involved. I enjoyed math growing up, so I thought teaching may be a possibility. In college, I had test takers and note takers to do everything for me, so I don't know what made me think I could teach. Though I couldn't write, nor pass out papers, nor correct papers, like everything after my accident, I adjusted my expectations and approach, and teaching really worked out.

My first time in front of a classroom was an internship teaching once a week at an elementary school. I was very nervous leading up to my first day. In college, I could hide in the background, but now, as a teacher, I had to be the center of attention. I remember waiting terrified outside the door, thinking, *These little kids are way more intimidating than adults.* I could only imagine their questions, "How do you do this? How do you do that? How are you going to teach if you can't even write?" These kids were going to think I'm a freak. "How is this person in a wheelchair going to teach us?" I was asking myself the same questions. I also worried about what I would do if I needed something. At home, there was always someone around. I figured elementary kids would have no idea how to help me, even to get me a simple glass of water. As the door opened, I prepared for the worst.

The moment I saw the look in the children's eyes, my fears vanished. They weren't afraid of me, as I anticipated. Every student's eyes lit up as if I were a Disney character and my wheelchair was a scooter. Their excitement quickly turned to curiosity, and they started to ask me questions. Two questions from that day have always stuck in my mind. The first was from a boy asking, "Why don't your legs work anymore?" The lead teacher felt embarrassed by the question, but I assured her it was not a problem and started to explain. I told them how I broke my neck, and unfortunately, that meant certain parts of my body didn't work anymore, including my legs. I'd concluded, "There are parts of my life that are difficult, but the way I look at it, it is not so bad, and at least I get to drive around in this cool wheelchair." I wanted to make sure they understood I'm still okay even though my body doesn't work the same.

The kids knew that it was a hockey accident that landed me in my chair, which prompted the second question, "If you didn't get hurt, do you think you would have been a professional hockey player?" I paused for a moment and thought about my answer. When I did play hockey, I was pretty good for a local high school player but recognized that I would never become a professional. That day, though, I hearkened back to another 1980s movie. At the end of the movie, *Dumb and Dumber*, Jim Carrey's awkward character pulls up to a broken-down bus filled with beautiful women. Carrey's character asks one of the women, "Do I have a chance with you?" She replies, "Yeah, there's a one-in-a-million chance of that happening," to which he responds enthusiastically, "So you're telling me there's a chance?" That scene prompted my answer: "Anything is possible, unfortunately I'll never get to know."

Very quickly, the internship became my favorite day of the week. I found it very easy to explain to the students how my life was different—that I needed help with certain things each day, but how, most of the time, my life was just like theirs, with family and socializing, activity and routines. I also witnessed each week the pride that the kids had when they helped me open a door or get a sip of my drink. They seemed fascinated that I was different. The kids were brave enough to ask the questions that adults think about when they see somebody like me. I'd explain when my way of doing something was unlike theirs. In turn, they got to play an active role in assisting me with my needs. Their innocence helped me look at myself anew and realize it was actually okay to be different. I noticed that I could make a difference in these kids' lives. My wheelchair was an obstacle, yes, but there was a way to teach from a wheelchair, and I could adapt anything necessary to help kids learn.

Even after that first positive experience, getting comfortable in the classroom remained a hurdle. I still had more questions than answers about how I was going to function in a classroom by myself. I worried about all the things that could go wrong with my body without warning. Spinal cord injury means losing control of your bodily functions. If you took a poll of SCI patients asking what they most focus on each day, two words would inevitably emerge: pee and poop. I'm not mentioning this to be crass. The status of my bladder and my bowel really is on my mind constantly, day and night. Of all the issues that can arise due to spinal cord injury, these two areas need the most attention and often when we least expect it or want it to happen.

Indeed, it was fair to worry about my body's impact on my teaching career—I experienced what was possible on one of the first days I was ever on my own with a class. It was my second year of college, and I was a substitute teacher at one of the elementary schools in town. I taught a group of second grade students. (Incidentally, I saw those kids graduate years later as their high school teacher.) I felt pretty good but apprehensive about being on my own. When the kids came into the classroom, they could not take their eyes off the wheelchair nor the man sitting in it. I figured I would let them get comfortable by asking some questions and getting to know me a bit. I drove my chair back and forth in front of the class, and their eyes followed me like a crowd at a tennis match. Just as the kids began to relax, my leg shot out and my shoe went flying across the room.

Another side effect of living with paralysis is muscle spasms, the involuntary movement of a muscle. When you are a quadriplegic, spasms happen without warning. That day, I had on a pair of my father's gray cockroach-killer dress shoes with silky socks—clearly a recipe for disaster. I'm glad those shoes aren't around anymore, as I came close to taking one of those kids' eyes out! If you thought the kids looked at me with wide eyes before, now they were frozen, and every mouth was open. I had to act quickly. With a smile on my face, I said, "Whoops, there goes my shoe!" What was I supposed to do? I asked one of the kids closest to my shoe to grab it and bring it up to me. The little boy was apprehensive at first, so I tried to assure him. "Don't worry about it. They are new shoes. I don't think they smell too much." As we went through our reading and math lessons, the first part of the day was going well. Each kid looked at my sock, as I drove up and down the aisle, but eventually, they stopped noticing the missing shoe, and the day progressed.

Having experienced what I have over the last thirty years, there isn't much that would embarrass me anymore. Anything that happens with my bodily functions is not something that I can control, so why be embarrassed? I also find that if I am comfortable with what happens, the people around me are more comfortable. Something like losing my shoe is an oops, and we go on with the day. As it turned out, the shoe incident would be minor compared to what happened later that day. Again, when your body has a mind of its own, it's not a matter of if but when the next thing is going to happen.

Autonomic dysreflexia—something you'd probably never hear unless you have been around a spinal cord patient. I sweat only in the part of my body where I have feeling and function. It is my body's reaction to, and warning of, pain and trauma. For example, I can touch a hot surface and not realize it until my body reacts—I have several burn scars to prove it. I experience the same feeling when something is going on internally. When it happens, how I sweat helps me analyze what is wrong. When I sweat on the left side of my face, there is an issue with my bladder. Sweat going down the back of my neck usually means I have a bladder infection. Sweat on the right side of my face tells me a body part has been in an awkward position for a long time. If my toe gets curled in my shoe, I do not realize it right away. It may be a half hour or an hour later when I start to sweat, and relief only comes when I have removed my shoe.

Any person with SCI knows that when symptoms come on, the first thing to do is check the bladder or bowel. A bit later that morning, I felt myself start to sweat, and my head started to pound, indicating a rise in blood pressure. I knew what this meant, and I knew it wasn't going to be good. I started pleading with my body, "Not now, please, not now." But it happened just before lunch. I could feel my body signaling that I was going to have a bowel movement. As minutes passed, the feeling subsided, which meant one of two things. Once in a while, it can be a false alarm, but it ended up being number two. Literally.

What could I do? The same way I felt, "Oh well, my shoe fell off," now it was, "Ah well, I pooped my pants." I did a sniff test and didn't really smell anything. I thought maybe I'd gotten lucky. There was only about an hour until lunch, so I taught the rest of the morning next to an open window to bring in some fresh air. Luckily, it was not a freezing winter day! I had no way to get in touch with someone to help me without going to the office, and I knew that Jeff would be coming soon to help me urinate with a catheter. I was sure to keep the kids in their seats and away from me for the rest of the morning and sniffed continually, hoping the kids could not smell much.

At lunch, I had Jeff check me, much like someone would check the diaper of a baby. My instinct had been right, so I asked him about the smell. At that point in my life, I was young and stupid—there's no way I would condone teaching through those circumstances right now, but I didn't want to leave. I didn't want this to be my first experience as a teacher. And it does make for a more interesting story, if not so inspirational. Jeff and I sat there for the next few minutes trying to determine if second graders would be able to smell me. After we were sufficiently convinced that the odor was not bad, I went back into the room. The day actually went pretty well, considering the two mishaps. As I drove home, I remember thinking, *If I could teach through that, I don't think there is anything in the classroom that I cannot handle.* There never was a more harrowing day in the classroom. In fact, school became my comfort zone.

The circumstances of receiving my first full-time job could not have been more ironic. My high school calculus teacher was named Mr. Waka. He had actually come to teach me in the hospital so that I could graduate on time. When I graduated from college, he was still working at the high school, even acting as the teachers' union representative. Especially during the summer months, he would ride his bike back and forth to school, easily a fifteen-mile ride each way. One day late that summer, he was struck by a car only about a quarter mile down the road from the school. He was thrown from his bike and, sadly, suffered a spinal cord injury.

The school year was to begin in less than a week. My former principal, Mr. Fabrizio, gave me a call and offered me the job. I felt terrible for my old teacher; how strange that it was this opportunity that arose. A week later, I began my career as a mathematics instructor at my own high school. A couple years later, I was even able to work with Mr. Waka when he returned to teaching.

I was going to be teaching at the school I'd graduated from four short years ago. There was a huge circle out front with a path cut down the middle. Students would park their cars in the parking lot on the opposite side and walk through the circle to enter the front door. I can't tell you how many times I'd have gone in and out of that front door, where there were two small steps up to a landing at the entrance. Two small steps—I'd probably never even paid attention as I passed over them in either direction. Now they prevented me from using the main entrance. When I got out of my van on my first morning, I had to drive my wheelchair along the side of the building, over a speed bump (which plays a role in my story a bit later), to the back of the school where the dumpsters were located. That back door was the only handicapped-accessible door in the building. The office was going to send someone over to open it, so I waited there next to the dumpsters.

I stared at the door for a while, until finally, a teacher passed by and let me in. The hallways were flooded with students at their lockers while I drove to my classroom. As I rolled, I could feel lots of eyes on me. At every turn, there were more students and more eyes peering at the new teacher in the wheelchair. When I eventually got to my classroom, the door was again closed. I waited there, trying to make eye contact with someone to help me open the door. Just like in college, I felt out of place. I was starting to worry about the day ahead, when a student noticed me sitting helplessly at the closed door. I offered, "Could you open the door for me, please?" The young student politely obliged and opened the door. I was assured enough to ask, "Could I bother you for just one more moment to help me with a couple of things?" She nervously agreed, not completely understanding what I meant.

I didn't like that my life was always about needing help, and especially with new acquaintances, there was usually apprehension at first. I recognized her awkwardness right away and wanted to make the situation as easy as possible for her, as I would for any person helping me. While mapping out my first day teaching, I began a conversation to help relieve her (and my own) nerves.

"My name is Mr. Maruzzi. What's yours?" I asked.

"My name is Samantha," she replied.

"What grade are you in?" I'd asked

"Ninth grade."

I could relate. "Then it's your first day of high school just like me. I just graduated from college, and it's my first day teaching. I was pretty nervous this morning on my way here. How about you?"

She nodded in agreement. As the conversation continued, I would ask her intermittently to put something from my bag onto my desk and move a few other things around to help me get ready. The initial awkwardness was disappearing.

I asked, "What are you taking for math this year?"

"Algebra," she replied.

"That is what I teach. You might just be in my class." I smiled.

After she opened my attendance book, I said, "That is good, thank you very much, Samantha."

"Is there anything else you need, Mr. Maruzzi?" Samantha had asked.

"No, thank you. Good luck on your first day. I'm sure we'll see each other again."

"No problem, Mr. Maruzzi. Good luck on your first day also!"

Her uneasiness had been replaced with reassurance in just those few moments, and she left the room with a smile. That brief encounter also relieved much of the fear I'd felt on my way to school that morning. Soon the bell rang, and sure enough, I saw similar looks of uneasiness as students passed by on their way to their seats. The second bell rang, and the students sat waiting for me to begin. I was determined to ease their fears as I had with Samantha.

"My name is Mr. Maruzzi," I said. "Welcome to my class. This class is probably going to be quite different from what you are used to. I'm sure a lot of you are wondering how I am going to teach you. It is true that there are many things in the classroom that I will need help with."

I continued to introduce the class and share more about my needs. As I was speaking, I noticed a boy in the back corner of the classroom. He hadn't interacted much with the other students when he entered the classroom. I got his attention and asked his name.

"Steven," he replied shyly, barely looking up.

"Could you come up here and help me at my desk for a minute, please?" I asked.

Steven reluctantly walked to the front of the room, looking down the entire way. He opened the drawer and reached into my desk to get the red folder full of worksheets that I needed.

"Could you count out seventeen for me, please?" I asked him politely.

He stood there counting sheets of paper with everyone in the classroom staring at him. When he was done passing them out to the other students, I asked if he could take the marker and write my name on the board. With the completion of each task, I noticed his confidence grow just slightly.

"Thank you, Steven. Nice penmanship!"

He smiled. "No problem. Anything else?"

"That's good. You did a good job, thanks," I reassured him.

He walked back to his seat standing slightly taller, with maybe a bit more confidence than when he had first come forward. Of course, I am not saying that passing out papers changed the kid's life, but it inspired some comfort, because anybody, even if just for a moment, wants to be needed and singled out in a positive way. It was evident to me that the act of helping me could be a great confidence booster for my students. As I continued with my classes that day, my own level of comfort grew alongside the kids'. By the end of the day, I knew teaching in a high school classroom was where I wanted to be.

September 1977. Elementary school. I wonder what the "second grade me" would have thought of the "teacher me?"

Chapter 7

Teaching More than Just Math

I loved that it was always, "Mr. Maruzzi, I need this," or "Could you help me with that?" From the moment I got to school, my mind and body were occupied the entire day. The feeling of constantly being needed was motivating and energizing for me. My wheelchair became, of course, a part of my classroom. Students caught on quickly that they would be required to play an active role in administering each lesson. The participation created a very interactive atmosphere, an unintended opportunity. Rarely did the kids just sit and listen to me lecture, passively learning. They were required to do all the things that I couldn't.

Our teamwork could only happen if the students had a level of comfort with my wheelchair and me. As nervous as I was early on, instructing and functioning interactively in the classroom came to feel natural right in sync with when living life in a wheelchair became second nature to me personally. The uncomfortable but necessary experience of college—and being out on my own as a quad—was now behind me. My situation required that I regularly instruct others to navigate my care in a step-by-step manner, which made for a natural transition to teaching mathematics. Problem solving was a way of life for me. And while I'd previously exerted a lot of energy trying to hide in the background—to not stand out—now I found comfort in a profession that required me to be the center of attention, sitting in the front of the room with everyone's eyes on me.

I realized that teaching high school students was a perfect fit for me, given their stage in life. In some ways, I will be eighteen years old for the rest of my life, frozen in time the moment my head hit the boards. The last time my life was like most people's, I was at the same point in my life as my students were. I had lived through adolescence normally, having the usual social and academic experiences throughout my teens. I also understood how extremely influential high school encounters and emotions can be, how they can leave a lasting impression. Like most teachers, the experiences and feelings from before my accident gave me a perspective similar to the kids that came into my classroom. What made my position unique was that I could also share perspective from a life nothing like what I thought it would be when I was their age. Through teaching, I could be a voice and an example for my students to find in themselves the strength they may need to overcome whatever obstacles in their lives.

That sounds cliché, and I suppose it is, like the mission of a motivational speaker. Remember those high school assemblies, listening to somebody who had suffered through adversity? Most students half-listened and generally left respecting that the story was sad but likely thinking, *That will never happen to me.* I didn't have a disability in high school, nor addiction issues, so I used to feel the same way—it was impressive for the presenter to have overcome obstacles and achieved personal accomplishment, but how was that relevant to me? I could never have imagined what it was like to live with a disability right up to the point when I had to. Now I had a unique perspective to share with my students—I was real life playing out in front of them, facing challenges daily. Compared to a forty-five-minute presentation or getting pointers here and there, appreciation sinks in when a child regularly witnesses and experiences life lessons in a relaxed atmosphere that allows students to be themselves.

For my students, there was more to my existence than helping me pass out papers and write on a chalkboard or, these days, a whiteboard. My students understood there were medical components that I had to take care of throughout the day. At least once a day, I had to go to the bathroom to get catheterized. A colleague who taught in an adjoining room volunteered to learn this process and help me. Now, it wasn't like I could plan to take care of it every day at 11:00, rather my body would tell me unexpectedly that my bladder was full. My classes understood that, when this happened, I needed to leave and get someone to help me, and they would be responsible for their own conduct. During these times, I never once had a problem with my class. The students gained understanding and respect for what I had to do, which brought out their best behavior.

Mutual vulnerability nourished these relationships. My students exposed their own vulnerabilities upon witnessing mine. I understood the impact I could have on the direction some students chose, and I looked at this as a very powerful responsibility. It was Spiderman's Uncle Ben that said, "With great power comes great responsibility." That is how I felt about the power I had, though I wouldn't compare myself to Superman or Wonder Woman. (I have to reference Wonder Woman—what boy who grew up watching Lynda Carter could forget her?) My superhero powers were more subtle, in line with the impact a puppy can have on someone. Imagine waking up one morning, struggling to get out of bed, unexcited but going through the motions anyway, when you hear something outside. You reluctantly open the door and find a cute little puppy. You'd of course pick up the fragile creature and bring it inside, making sure that it's warm and comfortable and has something to eat. You'd talk to the puppy and check on him every few minutes.

What you don't realize is that you are no longer thinking about your own day. You have seen life from the perspective of a helpless creature and have been able to make its life better. In turn, that makes you feel better about yourself, and perhaps that one small encounter could change the prospect of your day. Just about everybody understands the feeling of helping someone less fortunate than themselves. It is equally as empowering for the giver as it is for the recipient. I always noticed their gratification and felt their genuine compassion when people helped me throughout my day.

I was upfront about my circumstances with my students. As much as I wanted my students to see me engaging and enjoying life, they also came to understand that pain and inconvenience was a part of my existence. (In fact, many of them inadvertently learned what a bladder infection was through my acquaintance!) I didn't hide the fact that I would always live with hurt inside of me, but I've questioned, maybe that's the way it was supposed to be? We all have experiences that end in pain. Finding meaning despite pain from the past can be one of our greatest challenges. This is the message that I tried to convey to my students. There were times when someone would ask what it was like to live in a wheelchair. My immediate response was always, "I pray that you never have to find out," and while I'd never glorify my existence, I'd answer, "My wheelchair has never kept me from accomplishing something, except going upstairs."

When my students were comfortable letting their guard down, I recognized the look in some of their eyes. It was the same one I sometimes saw when I myself looked in the mirror. Behind those eyes lived a hurt that could plant itself deep inside, fester and, over time, poison the rest of your existence. I noticed how much energy kids exerted to create a public persona to cover up their feelings, something to take the attention away from what they perceived to be flaws when, really, these were attributes that just made them different. Universally, though it's a part of life, most students' conflict is related to feeling different in some way and having that exposed with harmful intent. The boy or girl who always got in trouble or who slept around wasn't doing it because they enjoyed getting in trouble or being known for deviant behavior. They intended to keep the focus on their behavior to mask confusion and insecurity going on inside.

Society sometimes looks at struggling kids as losers and not really worth the effort. Some are given that message at home, implicitly at school, and about everywhere they go. If you are told enough times that you are bad, you will start to believe it and potentially act accordingly. Whether it takes getting in trouble, turning to drugs or other tangible means to distract themselves from their reality, people are bound to try anything. I don't think it was "bad" kids that did these things. It was kids that had life kicking them so often that they got tired of getting up.

In a quiet moment outside of class one day, I was speaking with a girl who had a questionable reputation leftover from a party two years earlier. Her behavior had reinforced the notoriety. Being from a small town, my concern went beyond the classroom. When I asked her about her actions, she explained very simply that if peers were going to think her wild and promiscuous, she might as well act that way. Life allows kids to take any path, and the longer they spend on one track, the more difficult it becomes to change direction. Their very first obstacle is admitting to themselves that they cannot cope alone and finding courage to seek help. Even beyond high school, we may realize and accept the need for help, but the anxiety involved with actually requesting it can be overwhelming. Pride and vanity prevent so many people from admitting the need and accepting help.

Fortunately for me, pride and vanity are no longer a part of my life—it's difficult to be vain when you look like you have a bowling ball for a belly and no part of you is symmetrical (to use a mathematical term). It was important to me that my classroom was a place of comfort for all my students. Some of them had nowhere else to find peace in their day. I was able to build sincere relationships with my students, which worked well for both of us. I gave them instruction in math, and they helped with my needs in the classroom and generally in life—they touched me in emotional and human ways they may not have realized. Some relationships extended outside of the classroom as well. I was a mentor, a father figure, a positive influence for a lot of adolescents who did not have much direction in their lives at the time. I took a lot of pride in advising a student when they opened their heart.

These humbling opportunities with my students usually happened through simple everyday interactions. I often ate my lunch in my classroom, so that I could help someone with homework or prepping for a test. That meant I would need the student to help me too. Students didn't fully understand what it meant when they agreed. They made sure to take my sandwich out of the bag, unwrap it, and place it in front of me. I would say, "Thank you," and we would go on working, until the student would look at the sandwich, then up at me, and a light would go off. I would smile and say, "Yes! I need your help picking it up and bringing it to my mouth." Gaining exposure to what my life was like helped disarm the kids.

Helping me eat my lunch, correcting papers, opening a door, or any number of simple activities allowed me the opportunity to connect and reciprocate with enthusiasm and gratitude. You'll hear me repeat this, but I would stress to the kids that it is okay to admit to yourself that you need help. It is impossible for any of us to navigate every aspect of life without help, and more importantly, it is not a weakness to seek the help that you know you need. I am a living example. My wheelchair did not make me a better teacher than anybody else nor did it mean that I had a greater impact on students' lives, but it was a part of my life that I was honored to share if it encouraged their independence and confidence while around me. This is why I say, life in a wheelchair has provided me with unique opportunities for personal connection. I feel responsible every day of my life to be gracious and respect the generosity that people show me.

Some of my favorite kids were the ones who caused the most trouble. In fact, many teachers cringed when they saw certain names on their roster, but I saw opportunity. Living in the same town as I worked, I had acquaintance with the families of many students. I understood my colleagues' apprehension, but I never gave up on a kid because of their name or their past. In one case, there was a family of eight children who'd each come through my classroom, some on more than one occasion. I still know the entire family very well and will never forget the morning I found one of those kids sleeping on my heater when I arrived at school. She had gotten kicked out of the house the night before and had nowhere to go. She was in ninth grade.

Less than eight years later, I watched her graduate from Salem State College. It was in the same building as where I'd been injured and was my first time back since the accident. The ice and the boards were removed for the graduation ceremony. While watching, I realized that I was sitting in just about the same spot as I'd broken my neck. Crazy. The joyful feeling I had that day was an awesome and welcome contrast to my last time in the arena. Incidentally, every one of the kids from that family graduated and now have beautiful families of their own. I am very proud that I played a small role in helping them and many others find their way.

Addressing fears to become the person you know you can be is easier said than done. In encouraging resilience, I often suggested approaching small obstacles with attention and clarity. Minor successes on seemingly insignificant obstacles offer a roadmap to overcoming larger, life-impacting challenges. We can learn to address bigger obstacles before they get too overwhelming. Whether in a wheelchair or not, conflict is a part of life and how a teenager deals with it can have a significant impact on their future. If you really pay attention to screen images from the time kids watch Nickelodeon right through their TikTok years, conflict *is* entertainment—drama, fighting, chases, etc. Conflict portrayed this way is all about winning and losing, so, by high school, when personalities are exposed to a broad student body, competition is ingrained as the solution to conflict. "The only way my life can get better is if somebody else's gets worse." For most quads, words like *jealousy, hatred,* and *conflict* take on very different significance. My life can only improve when people around me play a part; we both benefit from the exchange and grow together.

I used to facilitate an activity that taught a peaceful, pre-emptive way to deal with conflict. Students of similar stature were paired and asked to stand back to back and join hands. Students would receive an M&M for pulling their partner's hand six inches forward. The object was to get as many M&Ms as you could in thirty seconds. Quietly beforehand, we would have paired one of the strongest kids with one of the smallest and given them instructions to review. Most pairs became competitive with their partner and treated the activity like arm wrestling. Inevitably, as pairs strained to pull against their perceived opponent, earning very few M&Ms, students would notice the big-little pair swinging their joined arms back and forth as fast as they could, with their M&M count increasing steadily. At the end of thirty seconds, the pair had over sixty M&Ms to share.

The exercise was a simple lesson in conflict resolution that demonstrated the value of a win-win situation: how much more reward we get working together rather than struggling against each other. I hoped the students would apply it to navigating adversity in their daily lives. Partnership and helping would be a much smoother path than conflict. The life of a quadriplegic yields this lesson daily: we understand there is absolutely no way to get an M&M without the help of another person. We also understand how influential we can be; our lives put all challenges in perspective.

Being in a wheelchair did not make me immune to having kids misbehave or harbor bad feelings toward me. I remember a time toward the end of school when I had to inform a student that he wasn't going to make it, as he had failed my class. He was a troubled kid who often had issues with other teachers. His grades were not very good, he wouldn't do much work, and it was hard to figure out how to motivate him. He even caused trouble with other students in the class. On several occasions, I'd had to speak to him about his behavior and even had to impose a detention and a suspension. His anger showed in his day-to-day demeanor.

It was a half-day after our final exams, and by 10:30 a.m., the school was virtually empty except for teachers. He strolled into my classroom with hope in his eyes that he had done well enough on the exam to pass and move on to his senior year. When I told him that he hadn't, he was visibly upset. We had a short discussion, and he lost control. I tried to explain that the accumulation of what he had (not) done throughout the year caused the problem, but he wasn't hearing any of it.

"F—— this school," he'd yelled, as he left the classroom and slammed the door behind him. Now I was faced with two problems: I had to address his behavior, and when he closed the door, I was trapped in my classroom.

Ours was a very old school, built in the 1950s, and I had no way of opening the door, but eventually someone did pass by and opened it for me. It was summer and sunny, so I'd planned to get outside for a while before I finished correcting exams. The town had finally built a ramp, so I could get into the school via the auditorium (no longer by the dumpsters!), but those particular doors were not built with wheelchairs in mind. To get through, I had to be extra careful, because I just fit. I was usually very good at navigating through, but that day, my joystick hit one of the door's handles, which sent my front wheels shooting up in the air, and my chair tilted way back.

If I hadn't had my wheelie bars to prevent it, I probably would have fallen completely backward.

A student was sitting outside and witnessed the ordeal. He leapt to his feet and ran to assist me. After we got the chair straightened out, I realized that it was Chris, the student that I had confronted a short time earlier. He was focused, made sure that I was okay, and I could see concern in his eyes. The incident was grounding and allowed us the chance to talk about his situation. We came to an understanding about why he hadn't done well in class, and I committed to doing everything I could to help him change his behavior, if he wanted it. We discussed how his behavior was ultimately only going to hurt him. He could be angry at the teachers or anybody else, but at some point, he had to take control and make decisions that would improve his life. We became closer as a teacher and student, and he went on to graduate successfully. It wasn't a single conversation that turned him around, but I got the chance to see his heart, who he truly was, rather than the person who had stormed out of my classroom only moments earlier.

I made mentoring a priority as an educator and as a human being. There were countless days that my students motivated me without even realizing what I had going on personally. To reciprocate, I helped others find motivation through me, someone who faced unusual conflict every day of my life. As I've mentioned, my condition gave me the opportunity to impact their lives in a different way than most other people could. As dark as it seemed behind the eyes of some of my students, whether known troublemakers or those who simply felt out of place, kids exposed who they really wanted to be in my presence. It was clear they didn't know how to get there, and I had the power to boost them up. I didn't paint a slogan across my chest, but day-to-day interactions enabled me to regularly influence and encourage resilience in the face of adversity. This connection became the most gratifying part of my job. I'd taken advantage of the opportunities God put in front of me and found my purpose.

September 1987. My senior yearbook photo. I thoroughly enjoyed my high school experience, aside from the obvious.

CHAPTER 8

Adventures in Teaching

Sometimes in life, we laugh, because we may just fall apart if we don't. I found strength in the humor and the irony that accompanied many of my experiences. There was a time that a fire truck pulled up outside my parents' house to tell them I had broken down and needed a lift. In my chair, I could navigate a lot of the small streets where I lived, so I would make my way around town independently. On sunny days, I would visit a family member or a friend or drive back and forth to work. I knew which roads were smoothest or the safest to get around. Some spots required that I become a bit of a daredevil—one was part of most trips I wanted to take. With no sidewalk available, I had to cross a bridge and drive on the street alongside passing vehicles through a three-way intersection. I had actually thought this would be one of the worst spots to break down—it would disrupt traffic in three directions.

That's exactly what happened one sunny summer afternoon. There was not much traffic that particular afternoon. Once I realized I wasn't moving, it took a couple minutes for anybody to drive by before I noticed a fire engine coming my way. I was out of college and in my mid-twenties at that point. Several of the firefighters were my age—we had gone to high school together not too long ago. I had a big smile on my face when they approached. One of them leaned out and kiddingly asked, "What's the problem? Did you break down?"

The widening smile on my face told them, "Yes, I did."

Once they realized I was serious, there was a laugh at my expense, and they went into action. One of the trucks stayed behind and directed traffic around me, while the other drove the half mile to my house to tell my father to get my van and come pick me up. I could picture my mother's alarm when the fire truck pulled up: *Michael needs help!* She'd have had a nervous breakdown before they even got to the door. The whole situation was hysterical (to everyone except my mother).

Humor does depend on a person's perspective. My students were witness to many of my wheelchair mishaps and appreciated humor, as did I, where a less familiar onlooker might be appalled. I told my students tongue-in-cheek stories about my surviving "dangerous and life-threatening" situations. Sometimes, I'd act shocked at their amusement. Here's how one story went...

"When I opened my eyes, I saw snowflakes. I was not excited," I'd started.

My students knew as much as anybody how much I disliked the cold. The building that I taught in was so old that, depending on which room you were in, it could be either 85° or 58°F. I preferred the higher temperature. In fact, the only time I ever raised my voice was if someone attempted to open the window without my permission. Cold and snow are two of my least favorite things. (But I *did* like a parking lot covered with about an inch of snow. It was the perfect time to race my chair at full speed, turn hard as my back wheels spun, and slide across the parking lot. Once or twice, the front bumper of a parked car was what stopped me!)

In my story, I was describing the prior afternoon, when light snow was in the forecast, and I told my students the details:

> I had to get my grades done, so I stayed at school until about 3:45 p.m. (when, in January in New England, the sun would begin to set). I'd decided to take a shortcut out the side door and down the alley, toward the front of the school to meet my ride. This way, I could spin my tires in

the snow on my way to the front of the building. (Not all choices are good choices.) The hallway was empty when I drove from my room to the door by the janitor's office, which led out to the side parking lot and alleyway. The door was old, and I could open it myself by backing in to release the lock and push my way outside. Once outside, there was more snow on the ground than I thought. I started asking myself whether this was a good idea but lost the choice when the door closed behind me.

I wheeled myself down the alley toward the front of the school, when I hit the speed bump—not facetiously, in fact, literally! I sat atop the bump, my chair frame slightly lifted and both my front and rear wheels barely touching the ground. I spun my wheels forward and backward continuously for a few minutes, trying to wiggle as much of my body as I could. I was not successful, so I stopped. I was experiencing what I had learned in physics: snow does not offer a lot of friction.

"Michael, what are you doing?" I had asked myself aloud, a trait I inherited from my father who still talks to himself in the third person on the golf course. I realized how pointless my efforts were.

In the middle of describing my escapade, I heard laughter from a student in the front.

"Are you laughing at me, Brittany?" I asked, pretending to be shocked that she was laughing when I was in such harrowing danger.

"No, Mr. Maruzzi. I'm not laughing," she replied. Brittany had the most infectious laugh, and once she started, she couldn't stop.

But I went on, over-embellishing, of course, and trying to hold back my own smile.

I could see the front of the school; it was about two hundred feet away. From where I was perched, I had a partial view of the parking lot. My van was probably waiting in front of the school, not in my view. Jeff had no idea I was coming out this exit. At this time of day, I knew nobody was intentionally coming down this alley from the front of the school. It was just dark enough that it was difficult to see where I was from that distance. No one was coming from behind me anytime soon either. As I sat there getting covered in a blanket of snow, all I could think about was how ridiculous I was to have gotten myself into this situation—what I must look like!

I sat there by myself, laughing aloud at my predicament. As the sky continued to get darker and the snow continued to fall, I accepted my fate.

"Nobody knows where I am, and nobody is randomly driving by here anytime soon."

Once again, there was a snicker from the class as I told my story. I smiled and looked in her direction. "Do you think this is funny?" Once again, Brittany did everything to hold back.

"Not at all," she said through pressed lips.

I continued on with my dramatic rendition of the events.

I waited for what seemed like an eternity—which, in reality, was probably 10 minutes—then saw a light in the distance. I thought it was an angel. In reality, it was headlights. Somebody had come to pick up their child from school. The only kids that were still there would have been in detention—thank God for the delinquents. The driver parked facing directly toward me. I started swinging my arms back and forth to get their attention. I was saved!

By this time, Brittany was laughing out loud, and the rest of the class were cracking.

> Imagine how I must have looked to that poor mother waiting to pick up her child. Her headlights land randomly on a man sitting in the distance, waving his arms back and forth like a crazy person. Tell me that's not the last thing you would have expected to see had you been in her place?

By the time I described how the kind lady came to help me, the entire class was laughing, and I ended with a smile on my face, saying, "I'm lucky to be alive!"

I later heard that Brittany went home and told her parents the story, and her mother was shocked that the class was laughing at my expense. We were actually all laughing together...my relationship with my students had that unique component. Imagine being a teacher, standing in front of the classroom, and your fly is open or your skirt is caught in your underpants. Everyone would be embarrassed as you fixed the issue, and maybe the class would take a minute to settle down. For me, the Velcro from one of my braces grabbed my clothing one afternoon. My belly was exposed to the entire class. I was in the middle of explaining a math problem when a girl in the front row whispered, "Mr. Maruzzi, look down at your shirt."

I looked down and then right back at her. "Would you pull it down, please?"

And on we continued with the math problem. No awkwardness. There was no place for embarrassment in my classroom; the kids and I were a team.

My classroom was not just about imparting life lessons and entertainment. I actually love teaching math. Once again, I came to realize my disability could be a positive component of my approach. The most difficult aspect of my job was the fact that I could not write. If I were helping a student work through a problem, they couldn't just sit and watch me do examples. I used their hands as my vehicle to explain how to do something in mathematics. While I instructed what to write on the paper, it required their mind to focus on what they were doing. I found that it gave students greater depth in their learning. No matter what their level, from the smartest to the most challenged, all students had a want for learning and a desire for accomplishment. My favorite thing about teaching was seeing the student get it. It generates a feeling of pride and accomplishment, though on a very minor scale, that can have lasting effects on other aspects of life.

There were many moments that blossomed from the most unlikely scenarios. While teaching summer school, I remember going into a colleague's classroom to ask her a question. On my way out, a girl in the class caught my eye as I was driving past her desk. They were doing an assignment, and when we caught eyes, hers were full of confusion and fear. I paused and asked if she needed help. I mulled the question with her and saw the smile when she got it. After the class, I spoke with her and found out her name was Michelle. She was the most quiet, meek student. I offered to tutor her, to help her through summer school. Well, Michelle passed that course and grew out of that quiet, timid persona. She joined my regular class during the school year, so I could continue to help her and went on to graduate from high school.

I believe that, at some level, there is a way for every kid to learn, and I felt the same way about their becoming young adults outside of the classroom. Every one of them faced challenges and obstacles, some much more than others. I always tried to emphasize that they had control of their lives to overcome any of those challenges. I reminded them that, like myself, getting help was not a bad thing. Letting pride prevail and internalizing struggles because you don't want anybody else to know what you are going through can only be detrimental. As I've mentioned before, seeing my need for help every day and playing an active role in that help naturally emphasized the point.

These takeaways, the aha's, are why I loved those personal moments with my students: a small conversation as we walked to the office when someone was helping me get my mail or a tutoring session after school that expanded into a conversation about life. Those moments when students let their guard down and showed a vulnerable side motivated me on a daily basis to be there for them. My students likewise got me through days when I felt sick, was sitting crooked in my wheelchair, or any number of things that distracted me from comfortably living life. Teaching allowed me to put all of that in the background. Every day that I got up to go to school, I wasn't going to work. I was getting dressed to enjoy an experience that reflected that I still control my life, and I still have the ability to help others.

January 1988. Enjoying the sun at Club Martino (a.k.a. my Aunt Florence's house), my winter getaway.

CHAPTER 9

Feeling Like a Kid Again

Writing this book has helped me move through one of the darkest periods of my life. I have started and stopped many, many times. I have written and lived genuinely in the events that I described, while other times, honestly, I was lost on the inside. I've always known that I would find my way, but I never considered getting lost in the first place. After significant personal reflection and writing, completion of this book will mean I've both accomplished a personal goal and captured my truest reflections. I have been energized to embrace life anew. I feel a sense of purpose each morning the moment I sit up in my chair and push that joystick for the first time. My motivation is born from understanding and accepting my past, being humbled and focused on the present, and ultimately relying on faith to find hope in the future.

Now, I don't mean to paint an overly rosy, this-wheelchair-will-never-stop-me picture of my life. As I've said, if I had a choice, this is most definitely not the existence I would choose. While I have adapted and enjoy being a part of many experiences, there is always an emptiness inside that is a consequence of my injury. What I cannot do *is* a big deal and having to sit back and watch it play out in front of me over the years has been hard. I coached my niece and nephew's youth teams, which gave me great joy, but I never had the opportunity to play catch or swing the bat with them. There were annual alumni hockey games or golf tournaments, and backyard gatherings would often include horseshoe or cornhole games. I was always a spectator, which sometimes left me feeling sad and jealous.

Before my injury, being active was a way of life for me. In high school, I played a sport every season, did things with my friends, and joined various other school offerings. I hammed it up in class competitions and skits during the Thanksgiving Day football pep rally, one of my school's major traditions, and student-teacher activities were part of our spirit weeks, which I loved as a student. When I became a teacher, I had to sit back and watch, which was not an easy adjustment. I missed out on a huge part of building relationships with students. I internalized my frustration—it was not a big deal in the scheme of things, but I felt envious in the moment. At one pep rally, a group of teachers organized a flash mob for the whole staff to perform. I really wanted to be part of it, but I was never approached, and for whatever reason, I never gathered the courage to ask (they would have welcomed me with open arms). I remember being angry at myself for missing out on something due to self-pity.

Moments like these will always be part of my existence, but I do not allow them to linger. This capacity to focus on life in the present and leave past emotions in the past is another benefit of my condition. The instantaneous manner in which my previous life stopped required that I find a way to manage the emotions tied to life before my injury. I feel liberated by leaving my past in the past, the good things and the bad. When I truly lean into life in the present, which is most days, I feel grateful. Living in a chair has relinquished many of the day-to-day anxieties that bog down others. The majority of activity that makes up my day is beyond my physical capabilities. The few things that I am able to do for myself require significant attention and concentration. Focus like that needed to complete even the simplest of daily activities has shaped my overall perspective.

Here's an example. My aunt had a candy drawer in her home for as long as I can remember. It was the third drawer down in one of her kitchen cabinets, and each time I opened it, my eyes lit up. It seemed to be filled with everything you could imagine—a kid's dream. I decided to recreate that tradition for my niece and nephew and other kids that came to my house. I moved mine higher to make it more accessible. I still like candy and have grown to appreciate it even more because of the effort needed to get the tasty reward. The simple act of opening a drawer and pulling out a piece of candy is difficult for me. I have to position my wheelchair so that I can hook my fingers around the handle of the drawer and pull it open. I then use my arm and fingers as a crane, attempting to retrieve one precious piece of candy. I have no control of my fingers, so it takes me a few attempts to succeed, but the snack-size candy is the exact weight and shape for my limp fingers to hook and pull toward the edge of the drawer. I have to slide it up the side of the drawer with enough momentum to sweep it out, over my joystick and onto my lap. Needless to say, there have been times that I miss.

That was the easy part. I next slide the candy from my lap up onto my belly, resting it there for a moment to collect myself, then I slide it up my chest and into my mouth. Maybe you think this feels like accomplishment, but the most challenging part is still in front of me. The difficulty in opening candy bars is a crime to the disabled community. Packaging is made of plastic that is both slippery and difficult to tear, even with two working hands. I've gained prow-ess at tearing open challenging wrappers using my teeth and hands. Granted, it takes a lot of focus on my part—one false move and the candy bar goes tumbling to the floor.

Consider a neighborhood relay race and the concentration it takes an able-bodied person to fill a spoon with water or balance an egg on a spoon and rush fifty feet without spilling. This is the focus I need for many simple day-to-day activities. Incidentally, Reese's Peanut Butter Cups are not only the best-tasting candy but also have the most user-friendly packaging—a simple spot of glue on the back provides easy access to the goods. Kidding aside, it is important for me to do as much for myself as possible, both emotionally and phys-ically. Strengthening the function I do have allows me to accomplish feats such as opening a candy bar or brushing my teeth.

Independence has also been motivation for me to exercise the few muscles that still remain under my control. (Exercise gives me the excuse to eat what I want too.) I did not spend much time in the gym before my injury, as my 6-foot, 130-pound physique would attest—I could eat anything I wanted without gaining weight. By the time I was thirty, exercise was really required. What I can physically do with my upper body is limited. My shoulders and biceps are where I have the most control, so with that in mind, I explored different ways to exercise.

Using weights and exercise bands, I built up strength to pedal a three-wheeled handcycle. I would be lifted from my chair and strapped into the bike's seat, with my feet secured to foot plates. Once my hands were fastened to the hand pedals, a gentle push would get me going, and I would be off, my arms rotating in turn, the cycle moving forward. I wasn't using a joystick, and nobody was pushing me. I would feel the wind in my face as I picked up speed. I had enough strength to move myself. It was exhilarating! For the first time in my life, I actually enjoyed exercising.

I always wanted to get a tattoo, but never had the arm muscles to warrant one, so I set a goal to complete four laps around a track, the equivalent of one mile. My reward would be my first tattoo. One of my favorite places to ride was along the ocean bike path in East Boston, which neighbors Logan Airport. As the planes took off and landed, I would pretend to race them. The path ran along the beach and wound back in a loop, so I could measure distance by the number of laps I completed. Once I was strapped in and given a push, my goal was to complete one lap. Initially, I had training wheels disguised as another person who'd stay alongside in case I needed a nudge. To complete my lap, I would get a last boost down the final straightaway, and I'd start pumping with all of my energy and focus.

My one-lap finish line was my cousin, Billy. He would spend the day sunbathing on a lounge chair, listening to a book on tape. I knew that if I made it to him, I could rest and get a drink. I'd visually measure the spot where I could pause and glide through the finish line, like Lance Armstrong at the end of the Tour de France (though my body was all natural!). Every few weeks, I measured my progress in a time trial along a straightaway that was parallel to the airport runway and had a green municipal trash barrel at the end. That was my marker. I would pedal and pump with the aid of the ocean wind at my back. As the barrel started to get bigger, I would feel myself slow slightly, but I'd keep grinding. I would start talking to myself, "Focus, Michael, keep pumping. You can do it. Keep working." I spoke in rhythm with the rotations, sometimes peeking at the odometer, always flexing one of the three working muscles in my shoulder—the front, side, and rear deltoids. With each rotation, a single muscle would move the pedal a quarter turn, then my focus would transfer to the other muscle for the next quarter turn, and ultimately, I'd use my third and strongest muscle to pull the pedal backward for a few feet of momentum. I was not breaking any speed records.

There was a time that I heard other people coming up behind me. My competitive spirit kicked in, and internally they became my opponents. As I got closer and closer to the trash barrel, I could feel my lead on them shrinking. I couldn't let them beat me. They were right on my heels when I gave one final push and crossed the finish line. I was victorious! The straps prevented it, but if I could have lifted my arms in triumph, I would have. As I rolled along enjoying my achievement, my "opponents" passed by. There is nothing more disheartening than realizing your maximum effort is the same pace as an elderly couple pushing a baby carriage. I couldn't help but smile. The exercise eventually paid off: I toned up and felt comfortable wearing a tank top, showing off my muscles. In full disclosure, I did not ride a mile without assistance, but I still celebrated with a little ink. I proudly wear the tattoo on my deltoid. It's the Roman Colosseum with IX etched into its facade. Nine was my hockey number.

Needless to say, simple activities take great effort for me, and simple doesn't always mean inconsequential. We can focus on the big picture and lose sight of important, simple things along the way. I fortunately rarely face this dilemma. I once looked at my existence as a devastating tragedy with little prospect of a future. Though we try, it is hard to accept how little we truly control in the world. Worrying about what we can't control distracts us—even prevents us—from focusing on what we can control and what we can achieve. I still derive strength from my focus on independently completing everyday tasks. My seemingly complicated life is, to me, pretty simple. I have no more control of my body than I ever have, but I am in charge on the inside.

My ability to leave the past in the past has helped me replace many of the things I miss with a better version, made possible only because of my life circumstances. I'll share a personal tradition that's evolved to give you a flavor. In Italian culture, food plays a major role on any family occasion. When somebody had a baby, everybody in the family sent food. When somebody died, everybody sent food. Even when I'd visit a relative unannounced, the table would fill with appetizers in minutes. Naturally, food was a prominent component of every holiday, and Thanksgiving was my favorite. Growing up, my mom would prepare homemade apple squares days beforehand, along with homemade macaroni for my father's soup. My grandmother split major holidays between each of her three daughters, and Thanksgiving was the one when Nana Marie, Great-Auntie Betty, and Great-Grandma Lena (whom we affectionately called the three little soldiers) came to our house. Not one of them could touch the floor when they were sitting in our dining room chairs.

Beyond my father's homemade beef soup, the menu always included turkey and stuffing and every conceivable color of vegetable. String beans, broccoli, artichokes, yams, sweet potatoes (the difference between the two I don't know to this day), squash and potato croquettes filled every space on the dining room table (with both leaves in). After dinner, we would play the card game, Tripoli, to make my mother and grandmother happy. You could win seventy-five cents if you were lucky. We would later have coffee and my mother's homemade desserts: the apple squares, lemon meringue pie, Italian cookies, raspberry strudel, chocolate cream pie, and a big bowl of fruit and nuts, in case the sweets weren't enough.

With so much food, there was no shortage of leftovers, and the morning after Thanksgiving continues to be something I look forward to as much as the holiday itself. Pre-injury, I used to wake up and go to the refrigerator around 10:30 or 11 a.m., which was close enough to lunchtime in my mind. I would look for the leftover turkey, stuffing, cranberry sauce, mayonnaise, and day-old Italian bread, and I'd assemble the perfect Thanksgiving sandwich. The base slice of bread would be slathered with mayonnaise, then I'd add stuffing, to help soak up the mayonnaise, then the turkey, cranberry sauce, another layer of turkey, a little more stuffing, and finally, the other slice of bread. I'd set the toaster oven to 250 degrees and place my sandwich inside.

I used to sit and watch the toaster like a little kid staring at presents under the Christmas tree. I waited for the perfect balance, for the outside not to burn, but the inside to be heated through. I watched the bread start to turn that beautiful shade of brown. (In later years, making an open-faced sandwich this way heated everything perfectly.) When I took it out, I'd study it for a moment to ensure it was cut in the exact spot that would make for the perfect first bite. I would even figure out which half would give me a better taste of every ingredient, and I'd sink my teeth into the best sandwich I would eat all year.

Naturally, my Thanksgiving tradition changed after my accident—I would depend on others to prepare that sandwich for the rest of my life. What's awesome is that my tradition became a shared experience with my niece and nephew. By the time I turned thirty, I'd moved in alongside my sister's family, and the holiday was now at our house. We had a contemporary duplex with an automatic door (opened by pressing a button) to get from one side of the house to the other. For one of his early birthdays, I'd gotten my nephew a bed with a ladder and a slide. By the time he was five, he didn't even use the slide, he just jumped from his bed to the floor. I knew, because he would land with a thud each morning, then I'd hear the pitter-patter of little feet going down the stairs on the opposite side of the house. I'd hear the automatic door open, and he would run down the ramp, jump into my bed, and snuggle in under the blanket. We were the only two awake at that hour, and this was our time, lying together and watching *SpongeBob* on Nickelodeon—I could sing the theme song to you even today.

I was also a cool uncle because my wheelchair was like an amusement park ride. A small person could stand on the back and hold on to the bars as I chauffeured them wherever they wanted to go. Often, my niece, Kate, would jump on the back, put her arms around my neck, and squeeze for protection. My neck and shoulders are the only parts of my body that have feeling, so I loved it. We would ride around the neighborhood or sometimes just from one side of the house to the other. She was merely holding on to me, but each time she wrapped her arms around my neck, it touched my heart. My favorite picture in the world is when my niece was a flower girl, sitting on my lap during a family wedding. These happy moments are not about being in a wheelchair, but I would never have experienced them if my life hadn't turned out this way.

When they were old enough, my niece and nephew joined in on my day-after-Thanksgiving sandwich tradition. We would set everything out on the kitchen table, and I would explain how to construct three perfect sandwiches. Once each layer was placed properly and sandwiches were in the toaster oven, now three of us would sit and watch the window to make sure they didn't overcook while warming on the inside. When each looked precisely done, we removed them from the oven, put them on plates, and I showed them how to cut the sandwich carefully down the middle to set up for that first bite. We'd spend the next half hour laughing together and enjoying our brunch.

Never in those moments did I miss making my own sandwich or lifting it to my mouth to take a bite. Not once was my life about being paralyzed. It was about enjoying a moment of pure joy with my niece and nephew. In fact, that first year we made it together, the sandwich was better than any I had ever made for myself. Not being able to walk is on par with not being able to make a Thanksgiving sandwich with my own hands. To me, there is no difference. It's not losing one thing, rather it's losing so many things that has made my life challenging. But it's my reality, and if I spent time thinking about everything I can no longer do, I would never have time for anything else. Instead, I keep my head up for opportunities, free of worry about things I can't control. I choose to be active, I cherish my niece and nephew, and I continue my traditions in a new way.

When I think of pure happiness, it takes me back to Christmas as a young child and the anticipation the night before, waiting to see what Santa Claus was going to bring. All the bedrooms in our home were on the top floor. It was exactly five steps from my bed to the doorway and another three steps to the stairs. There were thirteen steps on the staircase down to the first floor and the family room was to the left, where our tree was every year. Christmas morning, I would have to wait until 7 a.m. before I could get out of bed to open gifts. My parents were very clear the night before as we drove to my grandmother's house to celebrate Christmas Eve.

Christmas Eve was always fun and boosted my excitement for the next morning. My grandparents lived on the top floor of a two-story building in an apartment that overlooked the street—we entered into a family room at the front, then walked through my grandparents' bedroom to get to the dining room, which connected to the kitchen. If you were in the family room at one end of the house, you could see through to the kitchen at the other end. My grandparents raised six children in this small apartment. My mom and her two sisters were the oldest and had families of their own at this point. (With my aunts, it was like having three mothers, which definitely had its benefits!) My three uncles were all single when I was young, which was an advantage to the grandchildren, because they would pitch in to give us each one big gift.

As with Thanksgiving, food was the centerpiece of our Italian Christmas, beginning with an enormous antipasto salad (which I never understood, because there was no lettuce involved), presented beautifully on the glass tray that was only out for the holidays. We boys had to take our dress shirts off, so they didn't get stained during dinner. We'd be eating macaroni in our undershirts while the two girls wore large undershirts on top of their dresses. After dinner, one of my uncles would dress up as Santa Claus and present gifts to the family. Each clean grandchild would sit on Santa's lap, pose for the picture, and get our big uncle gift. We'd spend the rest of the evening playing with the presents. I would fall asleep on the way home and be half awake as my dad carried me up the stairs and placed me on my bed with Roadrunner sheets and pillowcase. (I loved those—still do and had them for years!)

Christmas morning, I'd wake up to find I had an hour before I could go down and open gifts, which was torture for little me. I would spend the hour going up and down the stairs, figuring the quickest path to get from my bedroom to Santa's gifts, thus my step count earlier in the chapter. Eventually, I'd stick my feet through the railing as I looked down to where the gifts were. "What was in that big one?" I'd be sure to count. "We each have six." "Which one should I open first?" Then I'd hear a sound, get scared, and run back into my room. I would watch the clock; each minute seemed like an hour: 6:57 a.m., 6:58 a.m., 6:59 a.m., 7 a.m.

"Everybody up! Santa came!" I would yell down the hallway, knocking on all the doors. I would run downstairs and still have to wait another few minutes before everyone came down. "Hurry up, guys, it's 7:03. Santa came!"

My mother would sort out the gifts and sip her coffee as we each opened one at a time. I don't remember any of the gifts specifically, but I will always remember that unbridled joy and excitement as a kid, running up and down the stairs on Christmas morning.

Arlene and I spent Christmas 2021 in Orlando with our three-year-old grandson, Luca, who brought us that same enthusiasm. Luca has been around me enough that he is comfortable and likes to push whenever we go someplace together, to 'help my chair move.' I love encounters with children under the age of five. Unlike adults, little children let you know exactly how they're feeling the moment that they feel it. My initial encounters are usually met with fear—sometimes kids hug their mother closely or they're scared to approach me. Eventually, the hesitation subsides, and my chair and I become a novelty—children walk up to the chair themselves, touch the different parts, and explore. Inevitably, they arrive at the joystick, when I do intervene, so they understand its purpose and who controls it. Once their curiosity is satisfied, the chair becomes a source of entertainment.

Nostalgically, Luca enjoyed pushing my chair wherever we went throughout the week in Orlando. This innocent interaction started with my younger cousins and continued with my niece and nephew. Having all grown up around me, they considered my chair a natural part of who I was. The wheelchair was a brand-new experience for my grandchildren. Toddlers' authentic and spontaneous reactions are more comfortable for me than adults, who react more internally, understanding a bit more about boundaries. As with the rest of my family, for Luca, I have ultimately become Michael-with-the-really-cool-wheelchair. One of my fondest older memories at Disney was going on the *Toy Story* ride with my nephew when he was about the same age as Luca is now. I'd been looking forward to coming full circle and enjoying the ride with Luca, but the pandemic intervened. Experiencing this through Luca's eyes would have taken me back to being a child myself.

Happily, as an adult I have found an experience that brings me joy like that of the six-year-old me on Christmas morning. Santa Claus has been replaced by sunshine. Since the accident, whenever the thermostat drops below 70°F, I am cold. Living in New England made me dread winter, because it meant seven months indoors, huddled next to the fireplace. A major carrot that got me through each year was the first day of seventy degree weather in New England. In March each year, I would track the weather to see when the sun would be shining and it would be warm enough to sit outside. When I see a sunny forecast, the anticipation of being in the sun has had me counting down the minutes.

I purposely built the deck into the corner of my house at an angle to block wind from disrupting my morning sun time. I knew the perfect position to face the sun for maximum exposure. When I opened my eyes at sunrise and saw the sun shining through the skylight window, I'd look at the clock—only six thirty in the morning. Nobody would be arriving to get me up until 8:00 a.m. I would lie in bed and watch the clock, planning the steps needed to get me outdoors as quickly as possible. With each passing cloud, the sun would beckon me, and I'd challenge myself to wait fifteen minutes between glances at the clock. At 8:04 a.m., the door would (finally) open. Jeff would help me out of bed, knowing my exact intentions, and I'd be in the sun in record time. Feeling the warmth of the sun on my face relaxed my entire body. More importantly, the moment of peace settled my mind, and I would relax even more.

I craved those beautiful sunny days when I got a little time alone. The rest of a usual day at home was spent assessing my body and who I may need, for example, to help prepare my food, cut it, and clean up after I ate, run errands, help with a catheter, or place me back into bed. Who would have thought that an afternoon sitting in the sun, doing nothing, would become such gratifying, precious time? Now living in Florida, sunshine is in abundance throughout the year. The first thing I still do every morning is get outside to feel the sun on my face.

May 1998. My niece, Kate, was a beautiful flower girl.

CHAPTER 10

Somebody to Love?

I wore number 9 on the back of my uniform, and as a math teacher, odd numbers were a regular part of my livelihood. Being an odd number socially was another thing altogether. I first started to feel out of place when friends and others my age were getting involved in long-term relationships. When we got together as a group, we would be a party of five or seven or nine, always an odd number when I was there. Being the fifth wheel gradually wore on me. What's more, I could never envision myself in a romantic relationship. I figured, *Why would anyone want me?* I was fine with my life. I could live without that part—at least, that's what I told myself and anybody else that ever asked.

Last chapter, there was a part of those beautiful sunny mornings that I left out. While waiting for Jeff or someone to get me up for the day, my gaze would often rest on the empty pillow next to me. I would feel a small twinge in my heart—a feeling of sadness about my life alone—but I didn't often linger on it. Most of the time, I was able to focus my attention elsewhere, but an emptiness had started to grow that would eventually impact my joy overall.

I remember reading a biography about Michael J. Fox. He acted in the role of Alex P. Keaton on the 1980s show *Family Ties*. He was one of the top ten characters in television sitcom history and went on to star in the *Back to the Future* movies. In his book, Michael J. Fox talked about suffering through Parkinson's disease. He felt his pinky finger twitch on the set of *Back to the Future*, but it hadn't been a cause for concern at the time. That twitch had been an early symptom of the disease that would progressively affect the rest of his body. Like Michael J Fox's pinky twitch, the twinge in my heart on those sunny days was a signal that something was wrong. I was alone, but I convinced myself very early that a relationship was just not realistic. Women wouldn't be lining up to date a guy in a wheelchair, and I had no sensation or movement where I needed it to make me the object of somebody's desire. I didn't have a wonderful physique before my injury. Now I was self-conscious of my body on a whole different level.

Romantic relationships are often initiated based on physical appearance. Ninety-nine people out of one hundred would be attracted to Ted Bundy if compared to *Married with Children*'s Al Bundy or Cardi B over Aunt Bee. I don't mean to offend anybody by referencing a serial killer. Focusing on physical appearance and attraction is a part of human nature. When we see someone we are attracted to, we focus on traits that are personally appealing. We may need to work up the courage to meet, but we get a feeling of excitement inside, and the heart starts to pump a little faster. Everybody desires to be on either side of that scenario. Don't we all want to have somebody look at us and feel that same excitement? Well, I couldn't picture a woman seeing me and fantasizing, "Look at those footrests. I gotta get me a piece of that!" (I know, it doesn't play well in the imagination.) Sex appeal was not a part of my physical makeup, as far as I could reason. Again, have a look at my prom picture.

Of course, if that were the way the world worked, nobody with a disability or another physical flaw would find love and affection. I know they say, "As you get to know a person, you learn that physical beauty is only a cover for what is truly going on inside." Blah, blah, blah. Those of us with major flaws know it is not easy to attract somebody to what's inside, when what we have going on outside makes us stand out for all the wrong reasons. There just weren't many women interested or attracted to me. I witnessed my friends going out on weekends, spending time at bars. I watched the interactions, but sat on the sidelines. Never would I make eye contact or strike up a conversation with a female in that type of environment.

Even physical contact with women, for the most part, was unintentional. Spending a summer afternoon around a swimming pool, my cousin Stephen's girlfriend was lying in a lounge chair next to me, enjoying the sun. I had been transferred into another lounge chair, so I was lying at the same level, with my arms by my side. I closed my eyes, relaxed, and my arm slid off my chair and—this is God's honest truth—ended up on the breast of the girl lying next to me. She was startled, which in turn startled me, but she understood it was not intentional. I apologized and said, "Tell me if I enjoyed it, because I couldn't feel it on my end."

She was confused for a second, then said with a smile, "Of course you did!"

Despite the frailty and great uncertainty of my existence, I have long since come to grips with what my life entails. I have found a way to cope with what I have lost and to appreciate the opportunities that I've had and remain in front of me. In my twenties, I tried to convince myself that I could take the same approach with my heart as I did with my turkey sandwich. I figured I could find something to replace that part of my life, but I failed to realize an important difference. The other losses were a result of my injury while this wound was self-imposed.

Deep down, I knew my choice to avoid affection was doomed for failure. From the time that I was a little kid, I was a hopeless romantic and craved affection. I was raised in a family that expressed affection openly, so I was energized and motivated by simple human contact. Routinely, I was the one to initiate contact, throwing my arms around anyone in my family, another relative or close friend. As I started into my teens, those same feelings extended to girls. My first significant relationship started in tenth grade and continued throughout high school. I realized at a very young age that falling in love was something that was important to me. My friends would go out partying on Friday and Saturday nights, but I rarely went. My standard answer when they asked was that I had to go to my grandmother's, when really I was going out with my girlfriend, Sherry.

When I get together with my high school friends now, I listen to everyone rehashing the old days, parties and places they used to hang out. I wasn't part of those stories, which was okay by me. I had memories that better reflected what I desired in life at the time. At fifteen, Sherry and I would go out, maybe for an ice cream or to see a movie, and we'd end up back at her house to watch television in the basement. That was where we spent a lot of time. Even before my injury, I was never a fan of the cold weather—I had my own blanket at Sherry's house decorated with Holly Hobbie characters. We went on special dates too—one of our best was a first trip to Boston to see *The Little Shop of Horrors*. We took a wrong turn out of the parking garage after the show and ended up in what was called 'the combat zone'—not the best place for two teenagers on a Saturday night. Thankfully, we made it out alive. The proms and other milestones we shared together were a big deal, and those are memories I will always cherish.

After my injury, grateful for having experienced genuine love with Sherry, I rationalized that I could shut down that part of my heart as long as I was feeling fulfilled in other aspects of my life. I managed to supplant those feelings in different ways. I was active enough during the week that it was not a major concern for me, but on the weekend, I needed to fill the void. From early September through to the first week of February, I had a date every weekend with football. I watched college games each Saturday and professional football on Sundays. After the season ended, I turned to my famous girlfriends: Meg Ryan, Julia Roberts, and Whitney Houston.

There were certain movies that I watched often, great time-fillers for when I did not have football. I'm not ashamed to say that I enjoyed watching romantic comedies (aka rom-coms). When scanning channels, I would stop for *Pretty Woman* or *When Harry Met Sally*. I can remember sitting back comfortably, as Richard Gere gallantly rose through the roof of his limousine, with Roxette playing in the background, his umbrella pointing at the sky in the direction of stunning Julia on the balcony, awaiting her prince, and I'd feel a tear roll down my cheek. I was a grown man crying, watching corny love stories. At the time, these movies fulfilled my romantic yearnings...I reasoned love was only one part of an otherwise fulfilling life, so consciously, it didn't matter much to me.

My choice to forego affection, however, started to infiltrate other aspects of my life. The first time I noticed a change in myself was nine to ten years after my accident, when my grandfather passed away. That day was a blow to me. It was my Papa Pelly's funeral, and I couldn't cry. I sat in the back of the church by myself, actually *trying* to cry. I thought about all the things we had done together, his hugs, and fishing. He and I would throw a fishing line over the bridge in Winthrop. One of the grossest things I've ever seen was him fileting a bluefish. Every Fourth of July, the whole family would gather to celebrate his birthday. It would be 95°, and we'd gather in the backyard underneath the peach tree, trying to find a little bit of shade. When I went to visit on my own, my grandfather was always waiting in a chair at the top of the stairs to his apartment. His eyes would light up, and he'd open his arms beckoning for a hug, smiling and laughing as he put his arms around me. He had a beard that he would rub on my cheeks like a Brillo pad. I will always remember that feeling.

The night of my grandfather's funeral, I couldn't explain my inability to express the emotions that I'd truly felt that day. I got back into the routine of my life and put the episode behind me, but it never stopped resurfacing. What was going on? I began to make note of other things. The affection and human touch that I once craved felt increasingly awkward and uncomfortable, so I intentionally avoided human contact. On New Year's Eve each year, I would discreetly disappear ten minutes before the hour, anticipating what would unfold at the stroke of midnight. Everybody would kiss their significant other and come find me, to make sure I didn't feel left out. It was an act of well-intentioned sympathy that made me feel worse. Watching people express affection became a constant reminder of what I was missing—my desire percolated to the surface more and more. I thought that I could experience relationships vicariously through others, but as much as I tried to live my life alone, I kept being reminded how wrong I was.

In my early thirties, I began to notice how little I had in common with the people around me. I had attended each of my friends' weddings, and they were all starting to have families. Naturally, when we got together, raising children and family topics dominated the conversation. Stories revolved around what was going on in their lives, but parenthood was another experience that I would never have. When we gathered at my home, I would usually leave my friends sitting around the kitchen table to go play with the little kids in the living room. They were laughing and joking, but I was not really part of what was going on.

It was really each night in bed that I started to harbor anger and pity. I would recollect every memory from the romantic teenage years of my life, convinced it would never be possible for me again, always blaming the wheelchair. I had a picture of Marilyn Monroe hanging above the door opposite my bed at home. There were many nights I would stare at that picture. Marilyn had everything she wanted in the world and still could not find happiness and peace in her life, a life that ended tragically but made her a cultural icon. I would say to myself, "I could have made her happy." My wheelchair was parked almost directly in view of the photo, which would snap me back to reality. "If only I were not in that wheelchair, I could definitely make a woman happy."

On the rare occasion that I tried to date someone, it did not go well, which only made me more self-conscious and stifled my confidence. The first time I became involved with a woman after my accident, I was in college, and my friends and I were caught up in our usual weekend routine. The boys would come to my house, hang around in folding chairs for a few hours, drink cheap beer before having to pay for them at the bar later that evening. I joined them out that night at a bar in Salem, Massachusetts. I did what I usually do and found a spot that I could back into, out of anybody's way as they walked by. From this spot, I enjoyed a few hours of people-watching as my friends attempted to pick up women at the bar. At some point, I noticed there was a girl looking at me. I didn't dare approach, and it was much too crowded to maneuver over to her. Surprisingly, she came to visit with me a short time later, and we left together.

Donna was a few years older than me and had two kids, a daughter and son who had Down syndrome. After spending a few weeks together, we went to the Topsfield Fair (a big state fair in Massachusetts) with her kids. Her son rode on the back of my chair with a big smile on his face as we made our way around. The following week, she came down with a bad cold. I thought it would be a nice gesture to send a dozen roses. The gesture must have been too much too soon, because that was the end of that relationship.

A few years out of college, I summoned up the courage to approach a woman whom I found attractive. We had gone out as friends periodically, but she was always involved in a relationship. There came a night that we planned to get together when she was actually unattached, so I decided to take a chance. Jeff and I had gone out earlier that day to buy one red rose, which I was going to surprise her with and express my feelings. I hid the rose so she wouldn't see it right away. I watched her park the car and heard her footsteps climb the front stairs. She walked in the door, and we caught up for a few minutes. I was getting ready to pick up the rose from where I'd put it, when she started to tell me a story. She had been secretly dating a man that she worked with, and now they were moving together to Arizona. Needless to say, I never brought out the rose and sat through one of the most uncomfortable dinners I've ever had to experience. After that, my confidence was pretty low, and the malaise slowly affected my attitude, even toward things that usually brought me joy.

For most of my thirties, I continued to balance the good with the bad. I had the inner strength never to give up on life, but by the age of forty, I'd gone from leading a life of purpose and joy to going through the motions and trying to get from one day to the next. It seemed like the shift happened overnight, but in reality, the choice that I had made a quarter century earlier started to take over my life. Each day became more difficult to focus. I had even lost some enthusiasm for my job, once my greatest motivation. I had an eye-opening moment with one of my student helpers while correcting some papers. The student was telling me a story about something going on in her life, but I was not there mentally. I'm not sure I listened to anything she was saying, so when she asked me a question, I had a blank look on my face. She followed with a serious brow, "That's okay, you don't really listen anymore anyhow."

I reacted with surprise and confusion. I knew what she said was true, but I hadn't purposefully thought about it. I had found it difficult to focus wherever I was because my mind was fixated elsewhere. For the longest time, my life had worked that way. I suppressed my true feelings and continued to find happiness. Looking back, the biggest mistake I made was keeping it all to myself. I never wanted to burden those close to me, figuring they had enough to deal with in physically assisting me. I could suffer alone. I was good at covering up so that nobody would really understand my inner turmoil. Still, I don't think anybody can live life without venting or having a sound-board to relieve internal frustration and fear. For me, there was one person with whom I felt comfortable expressing my feelings.

She had been a student when I first started teaching. For the purposes of this story, I'll call her Mary. Mary suffered from her own mental health issues, so I spent a lot of time tutoring and mentoring her through high school. Our mutual vulnerabilities deepened the connection. We continued to maintain a friendship for several years after she graduated. I had been a sounding board for her in high school and continued to be well into her twenties. Periodically, she would come by in the middle of the night, when she was having anxiety issues. It personally felt good that she needed me and that I could lift her to a better place.

At some point in my thirties, Mary became the person in whom I would confide and explore my consternation. To be honest, it was not very often that I did open up, even to her. Each one of my failed romantic experiences had reinforced that I never wanted anybody to have to live the life that I do. I felt no woman would want to be with me anyway. She heard me say this on more than one occasion. I would say it aloud to convince myself as much as her.

Mary would also tell me about her inconsistently successful romances. There was never a time that I felt our relationship could be anything but platonic. We remained close in every other way. A few years later, Mary met somebody, and they planned to get married. I had supported their relationship, as I was supportive of everything that she did in her life, and I attended her wedding. When I watched her say, "I do," true feelings bubbled up, and I found myself thinking, *I could have made her happy, if only my chair was not in the way.* In many ways, I looked at her the way I had looked at my Marilyn

Monroe poster. For me, the prospect of a romantic relationship did not seem like a reality in general. Not to mention that she was ten years younger than me and a pretty girl who could have any guy she wanted. She was way out of my league. Now she was happy, and I was glad. In fact, I was experiencing joy through somebody else once again.

A few years later, Mary's marriage was not in a good place. I came home from school one afternoon and found a letter on my kitchen table. I read the letter, which shared how Mary had been in love with me for a long time, but could never act on it. As I continued to read, my emotions overwhelmed me; I was in disbelief. She never acted on her feelings, she wrote, because "you always said you never wanted anybody to get close enough to you and have to live your life." The level of frustration and anger at my condition has rarely been greater than that afternoon, when my own words came back at me. I was sick to my stomach.

The next morning, a cold winter day, I was in my living room in front of my gas fireplace. I had been exercising to relieve some of my frustration. I remember being so angry at myself that I couldn't hold back my emotions. I turned up my CD stereo as loud as I could. The other side of the house was empty, so I was truly alone. The emotions that I hadn't been able to ignite for years suddenly burst out of me, all at once. I cried and kept crying—it was beyond me to stop. I screamed at the top of my lungs. "Why?" I screamed. And "why" extended to "Why me?" which ultimately extended to "Why me, God?"

This had not been the fault of my wheelchair. The misunderstanding had been the sad consequence of my choice years earlier to push everybody away from my heart. With AC/DC's "Hells Bells" blaring in the background, tears kept streaming down my face. I have never cried so much before or after that day (until my recent experience with Hurricane Ian). At the time, I couldn't believe I was where I was in my life. I hit a lull after a while and stared out the huge picture window over my fireplace. The cold blue sky outside was beautiful, and I realized I didn't want to be this person anymore. I didn't want to hide behind a pretense of happiness.

Unfortunately, the more I wanted to change things, the more frustrated I got that nothing was changing. In the months that followed, it felt like I was sleep riding through life. I still engaged in my daily activities, going to work, attending family events, spending time with friends and their wives, everything basically as it had always been. The realization that someone actually *had* had feelings for me was the event to push me to my breaking point. Looking at it even today, convincing myself that I was not worthy of love just because I was different is the one thing I regret in my life. I held on so tightly to that belief, for so long, that the only way to function through it was to dull my emotions. I didn't need alcohol or drugs. During those years, I transferred my time and energy into making the lives of the people around me better in any way I could.

June 2001. I have greatly appreciated the love and support my close friends have exhibited over the years. We have been in each other's lives since the age of five when we were rinky-dinks (ice hockey newbies).

CHAPTER 11

Time Is Something None of Us Is Promised

Throughout my strife, I was always able to express affection with my niece and my nephew. They became my only authentic distraction, so I took advantage of every opportunity to spend time with them. I mentioned that I was lucky enough to coach them respectively in softball and baseball. In fact, I led one of my teams to a championship against overwhelming odds. It was the greatest athletic achievement of my life, and I didn't do a thing. The other softball team had come into the championship game undefeated, and their pitcher was six inches taller than anybody on our team. It was supposed to be a slaughter. The game was at the local park down the street from my house. Fans lined up on the sidewalk along the fence to watch. As the game began, family members of both teams cheered on their kids. It seemed like more people came to watch as the game progressed, maybe because our team actually stayed in it. Last to bat, our best player was up. She hit a home run with a few runners on base, and we won the game! It was wonderful! That same year, the Red Sox won their first World Series in a century, so our championship was a bit overshadowed.

A few years later, I coached my nephew on a Babe Ruth baseball team for a couple seasons. We usually began at the end of April, right around the timing of school vacation. In Massachusetts, the first day of school vacation is also Patriots Day, when the Boston Marathon happens and the Red Sox have a home game. It was one particular Patriots Day, as I was getting ready to head to baseball practice, that I checked my urine tube and noticed blood. Blood in my urine meant a trip to the emergency room. Perhaps ad nauseam (maybe to give you a sense for my condition?), I have referred to the effect my bodily functions have on my day-to-day existence. I apologize, but here we go again. At least five or six times a year, I suffer from a urinary tract infection. I am unable to empty my own bladder, so by regularly inserting a catheter, bacteria is more easily introduced to my system, which leads to frequent infections. Most of the time, the doctor takes a urine sample, and antibiotics clear it up within four days. This bladder infection would be much more significant.

My father and I got to the local emergency room a short time later, around 3:00 p.m. A holiday in the hospital means that most of the doctors are not there, though one is usually on call in case of an emergency. Unfortunately that day, my urologist did not think my situation warranted his concern. I waited for a number of hours until a nurse finally got the doctor on the phone. He instructed her how to remove the Foley catheter tube from my bladder. When the tube was taken out, blood sprayed all over the emergency room. The nurse looked scared and bewildered, as if she had no idea what had happened. The infection had suddenly taken a turn that was anything but routine. I became nervous and hugged my father. I remember whispering in his ear, "Daddy, I think I'm going to die." I ended up being rushed to the emergency room at Mass General in Boston, and I was in and out of consciousness. My body had turned septic, meaning the infection had gotten into my bloodstream. My body had begun to shut down. The doctors were pulling blood clots out of my bladder.

I spent five days virtually motionless in the hospital, on heavy antibiotics to combat the infection. I went home with a PICC (peripherally inserted central catheter) line that would continue to deliver antibiotics directly to my heart. Three times a day, I was hooked up and administered medication through that line. Heading home, I looked forward to the comfort of my own bed, until I was undressed. Our norm was to check my skin daily, and this time, I had a pressure sore—there was a hole in my tailbone. I knew this meant I'd spend a significant amount of time in bed waiting for the wound to heal. Mentally, it was the last straw. For the first time in my life, I felt defeated. I literally had no choice but to lie in bed with my thoughts.

As much as I wanted to be left alone, it was not possible. I didn't interact much with family that came in and out to turn me every three hours. Everyone had to make sure there was food in the house and that I was fed. I couldn't be left alone. As I already felt like a burden to my family, this amplified that sentiment. Covering twenty-four hours a day, many people had to disrupt their lives to accommodate mine. Of course, I am grateful and blessed to have had family and friends around to take care of me (they were all living independent lives, which I wasn't lucky enough to have, I lamented back then). The mental burden I was putting on myself at that point had me spiraling downward. I lay in bed, facing one side or the other every day for eight weeks. The state of my existence was getting too much to take; even a personal DVD player playing the new show, *24*, starring Kiefer Sutherland didn't entice me. I was tired both physically and emotionally. *Why me?* At some point, I started asking God, "Seriously? Is there anything else that you have for me?"

My niece was about twelve years old at the time and came over from her side of the house one morning. She smiled at me. Despite my depression, I smiled meekly back. She climbed in the bed with me, and we watched TV for a few hours, talked a bit, and I actually ended up with a smile on my face. I was as low as could be, yet I was still motivated by her. That time with her triggered a shift in my thinking. I would need to find a way through this.

Having spent so much time faulting myself and questioning God, a friend convinced me to get my answers directly from the source Himself. "Volpe" is how teachers and students referred to my friend and colleague, Stephen. There should be a picture of him under any definition of a great teacher. I don't think I ever heard him raise his voice to a student, and he made a personal investment in each kid that entered his classroom. I'm not saying his room was perfect. There was an afternoon when, in the middle of class, I heard a ruckus going on next door in Volpe's classroom. Our rooms shared an adjoining door, so I had a student open it. Two girls were yelling at each other, inches apart. I didn't see Volpe until finally spotting him in between the two girls, trying to make peace—both girls were nearly six feet tall, and Volpe was five feet six inches at best! Order was soon restored. He used to hang on the back of my wheelchair with his rolling desk chair, and we would fly down the empty hallway. We had to tone down our antics when the principal's wife, who also worked at the school, turned the corner one day as we were passing. She looked at us like a disapproving mother. (The next day, the principal very politely asked us to stop.) Volpe was another reason that school rarely felt like work.

Right around the time that my life was fracturing, Volpe's wife was suffering through ovarian cancer. Witnessing the way that he dedicated himself to taking care of her was yet another example of his character. I noticed the strength that both his wife, Gloria, and he derived from God. After ten years, his wife lost her battle and passed away. One of the things Gloria had asked of him before she died was to not live life alone. A few years later, he met Dina, a breast cancer survivor herself, and they found something special in each other. They also shared their faith. When Gloria was alive, Volpe and his wife had attended a healing mass once a month. Volpe's life changes occurred right around the time that I was my lowest. Normally, my students inspired me to get through the day, but it was difficult to put on a brave face during that time. Volpe could see that I was not right. He suggested that I attend a healing mass with Dina and him. I agreed, but I'm a realist. I wasn't going to go into church, say a few prayers, and walk out.

I sat in the back of the circular church watching people file in and looking at the program. The music started, and the opening hymn played in the background as Father Ron walked in. He had a beard and wore a long white linen robe with a religious scarf around his neck. When he stepped on the pulpit, I noticed he was wearing a pair of sandals. In many ways, he reminded me of my aunts and uncles who grew up as hippies in the 1960s. When he introduced himself, his voice and demeanor matched his clothing. He had a wonderful ability to relate words from the Bible to what was going on in my present-day life.

The healing portion commenced at the end of the service. Since it was my first time, I stayed in the background to observe what was going on before involving myself. People lined up in three different aisles to reach the pulpit. About a dozen people would kneel at a time as Father Ron went to each one individually, quietly touching and praying for their healing. Family members or supporters also laid their hands upon the person receiving the prayers. It wasn't long before I was comfortable and understood what was going on. I assessed where I'd go to be the least burdensome. I saw a spot and, surprising myself, was confident enough to head down the aisle. What would I pray for? Throughout the service, Father Ron stressed how healing comes from the inside. I knew my heart was the most damaged part of me. I decided to ask God to help repair my heart.

Spring, 2002. Kate and Michael on our trip to Disney World.

CHAPTER 12

Waking Up to the Most
Beautiful Blue Eyes

When Father Ron withdrew his touch and completed the last prayer, I took in a deep breath and let it out. (Just in case, I looked down at my legs, but there was no miracle that day.) It didn't matter what condition my body was in, I would not be able to function properly with a broken heart. For a short time, I was motivated by the healing mass, but after a while, it seemed that not much had changed. Like anything else in life, the intention was great, but actually changing my life was a much more daunting task. For a number of years, I had directed anger at my chair as the culprit for never having filled that void. Whenever I considered romance, I anticipated the end before it began. I was convinced that a long-term relationship would not become a reality. This made the prospect of any relationship impossible. As I've mentioned, only years later would I accept that it was me, not my chair, that brought me to this low point.

I decided to examine the chain of events that began back on the campus of BU. After seeing the other quad twenty years ago, I had subconsciously planted a seed when deciding that I was undesirable. That seed grew, and when it ultimately blossomed, it was a foul-smelling, hideous flower rooted in the middle of my front lawn. My world had fallen apart as those suppressed feelings bubbled to the surface. Now, finding my way back would be a challenge.

Summoning motivation and energy can be difficult at such a low point in life. I thought about what I would say to a student in a similar state. The stark reality was that it was not something I could fix in a day, a month, or any set amount of time. I needed to narrow my focus and simply start in the right direction. I was finally at a point in my life where I was listening to my own message.

The first step was to open my heart, which I did. Trying to find somebody to fill it was definitely not an easy nut to crack. I wasn't going to become any better looking than I was previously. How would I sell myself? It was the technology era, so I gave computer dating a try. I had one encounter that we will call unsuccessful. After communicating online for a short time, we spoke by phone and arranged to meet at a nice restaurant in Boston. As our date approached, I couldn't remember if we'd talked online about my wheelchair, and I realized my profile picture was from the shoulders up. If you didn't know me, you may not have noticed the chair. A friend drove me into town and dropped me off outside the restaurant. I told her to wait nearby just in case—if this woman did not realize I was in a chair, she was going to be in for the shock of her life. The moment of truth came, and it was clear she didn't expect me. After an awkward dinner, I never heard from her again.

Building a relationship with me would be different from how it happens with everybody else—physically, I'm not anybody's dreamboat. In fact, my first interaction with my wife, Arlene, was more of a confrontation than an introduction. It occurred one winter after I'd come home from a vacation in Florida. I had been lucky to get some extra time beyond the regular school break to see a couple doctors and simply enjoy the warm weather in the middle of winter. I had to miss a week of school, so I'd made sure that my lesson plans were up-to-date and everything for the substitute teacher would be organized and ready to go. My main goal was to avoid any catastrophe in the classes during my absence.

Once back to school, I naturally asked my students about their math classes while I was gone. One class had convinced the substitute that I'd given them permission to watch *Harold & Kumar Go to White Castle*. I, of course, knew nothing about the movie, but learned it was rated R and thought, *Really? But who cares as long as nobody notices.* To my students, I had to be sure they understood they'd behaved wrongly, and I was upset.

"How could the substitute let you?" I'd asked in a stern, deep voice to emphasize my disappointment. They told me that Arlene had been the teacher, when I asked. I'd thought, *Who is Arlene, and why are they referring to her by first name?* It sounded a little strange to me. As it turned out, one of the kids in class, Giovanni, was dating her daughter at the time, so they called her Arlene as they did outside the school. (Now the young couple have wed and have two beautiful children, Aurelia and Gianluigi.)

The next morning, I saw a woman no more than five feet tall, barely a hundred pounds, striding down the hallway to confront me. Apparently, Giovanni had visited his girlfriend and told Arlene that I'd been upset about the R-rated movie. In her right hand, Arlene held a double extra-super-large Dunkin' Donuts coffee—the cup was almost as big as she was. As she came closer, I could read "I will show him a thing or two" all over her face. She started by saying, "The kids told me that you gave them permission to watch that movie, and it was inside your desk." As our heights were about the same, she looked me straight in the eyes when she spoke. I'm not going to lie…I was a little bit afraid.

A couple things struck me during that first encounter. One, don't mess with Arlene—there was a lot of fire in that tiny package. The second was her striking blue eyes. They were a shade of blue that I had never seen before (nor since, until I looked into the eyes of Gigi, Arlene's granddaughter). I soon learned more about Arlene. She was the cheerleading coach at the high school. She had four children and lived in a new house on the other side of town. I didn't interact with her much after that initial encounter, sometimes seeing her around the building if she filled in for another teacher. On the first day of school a few years later, the entire staff gathered in the library, as was our norm, for the principal to introduce new teachers. I noticed the Dunkin' Donuts coffee cup bounce into the room, followed by Arlene, who was holding it. Arlene stood up when they introduced the new staff, and I learned she was going to be helping in the math department.

I was accustomed to having paraprofessionals assigned to my classroom as a liaison for students on individual education plans. They almost always started by telling me they didn't know math. I noticed right away that Arlene knew mathematics, and she took notes every day. We learned to work well together, and she was great with the kids. Students often went to her for assistance, even if they weren't assigned to her. She made every effort to help kids in and out of the classroom. Considering all the years that she worked, there are countless students who can thank Arlene for getting them through a math course or the standardized state test. I requested her every year after her first, as did many of my colleagues. We all appreciated how much value she brought to the classroom, both for the teacher and the students.

Aside from her abilities in math, I first liked Arlene because she was always bubbly and brought a relaxed atmosphere to the classroom. Her rapport with the kids was natural. She understood what high school kids were going through, having four children of her own and two of them in high school. From the moment the bell rang, you could see her flying up and down the hallways. Arlene also spent time in English, Science, and History classes, so she moved fast—sometimes, you could feel the breeze as she passed. Every kid knew Arlene would do anything for them during the school day, but when the bell rang at 1:50 p.m., they also knew she would be the first one out. She would want to "rip a butt," as her children would say, referencing cigarettes, but she had to drive them all to their extracurricular activities, prepare dinner, and do everything else a mother deals with on a daily basis.

Arlene and I spent a lot of time together during the school day. We struck up a nice friendship, and I enjoyed it when she was in my classroom. She never went to extracurricular school events, so apart from her kids there at school, I knew very little about her. In fact, she was very private about her life. A few years passed, and Arlene's older kids, Santino and Micayla, graduated. Janel and Pasquale, her two younger children, were nearing graduation. Arlene was now spending most of the day in the Special Education classroom across from me. Each morning before school started, instead of turning left into my classroom, I made it a point to turn right and say hello to Arlene and Miss Ball, another paraprofessional in the building.

The school's classrooms had heavy wooden doors with a small pane of glass to see through. Each morning, I would bump their door into the cabinet on the other side, announcing my arrival with a bang. We'd sit together for a few minutes, discussing school gossip and life in general. I incorporated humor every morning, because I liked to make Arlene smile. I would bring my standard bagel with cream cheese, and Arlene would help me eat it as we talked. She also helped me straighten out, whether it was fixing my collar or making my pant legs uniform on both sides.

After a while, I noticed something different about Arlene. I don't know when it happened specifically, as it seemed to be a gradual change. She had lost her bounce. Arlene especially always had energy and enthusiasm, but the positive aura she carried with her was fading. While she was still very good at what she did, she wasn't completely present, or at least in the same way she had been. She shared her beautiful smile less often. I noticed when she stood next to me in the classroom, she'd sometimes hold my hand inconspicuously. It seemed that she was gaining comfort in holding my hand, so I would casually let it fall by the side of my chair. What struck me most was her eyes—that spark that could light up a room had been replaced by melancholy, even emptiness.

Whenever I asked if something was bothering her, she'd quickly respond that everything was fine, though I was never convinced. Around that time, interestingly, I noticed that the touch of her hand created a surprising and unfamiliar sensation in me, which I could not ignore. When people lose a part of their body, like a leg or an arm, or lose feeling like a quadriplegic, they can experience "phantom pain" below their level of injury. From the time I was first in the hospital, people have touched my legs and asked, "Can you feel this?" showing disbelief when I shook my head. I also have no feeling in my hands, having burned them several times over the years as evidence. Yet when Arlene held my hand, it felt like she was rubbing something gently on my palm, like a pebble or paperclip, and I could feel it.

I remember asking her, at one point, if she was scratching my hand.

"Yes, I am," she'd said, with surprise in her voice. "Is that okay?" She'd asked as if she were doing something wrong.

"Of course it is," I'd replied. "I can tell when you are doing it, funny enough. The sensation runs right up my arm."

She had smiled at me for a moment, but the smile was gone almost instantly.

Arlene functioned through each day without her usual enthusiasm, until one afternoon when I saw the depth of her sorrow. There was an unused student bathroom near my classroom, for which I had my own key. Access allowed me privacy to take care of everyday medical procedures, like catheterization and draining urine bags. A few of the teachers, including Arlene, had voluntarily learned how to help. Arlene was usually in my classroom or across the hall, so her help was convenient, and she seemed willing whenever I needed it. On one of these routine visits, after she had closed the door behind us, her eyes filled, and she began to cry almost uncontrollably. I sat and comforted her while she released emotions that apparently had been buried for a very long time.

No matter how strong the person, sometimes, we can't see a path forward and become overwhelmed. This is what was happening right in front of me, and I don't think there was anything I could have said to make her feel better. Arlene kept apologizing for getting so upset, but I reassured her not to worry about it. At the time, we never discussed the details of what was going on, but I told her I would be there if she needed me. Unfortunately, it was just a couple days later that the severe bladder infection landed me in the emergency room. I ended up missing over two months of school.

Weeks after my release from the hospital, I was able to sit in a reclined position in my wheelchair for a few hours each day. I was relaxing outside on a sunny afternoon, when I got a phone call. I didn't know the number, so I answered hesitantly, but I recognized the voice instantly. It was Arlene. She spoke very timidly.

"I got your number from Mr. Webb. Is it okay if I come visit for a little while?" she had asked.

"Of course!" I replied quickly.

She was right down the street and pulled into my driveway less than thirty seconds later in a large white SUV. The door opened, and tiny Arlene got out of the huge vehicle. At this point, a Dunkin' Donuts cup was understood to accompany her, and, yes, she had the biggest one they sold in her hand. I noticed immediately that she had on a dress. At school, she always wore a pair of pants with little flat shoes. The contrast made the dress that much more noticeable. She had a smile on her face as she walked quickly up the ramp to the deck. She asked how I was feeling. I told her I was looking forward to getting back to school.

The conversation became personal rather naturally after that. Arlene said she'd been nervous to come by, not wanting to bother me. I assured her it was no bother. She went on to describe personal experiences from her past. As she spoke, I realized the feelings she was navigating were some of the same that I had experienced throughout my life. The look in her eyes was the same one I'd been seeing in the mirror for a time. I could sense that she had been struggling for a long time. While the details of Arlene's story are unique, she had, like me, always put her needs on a back burner to make everybody around her happy, especially her four children. Arlene's feelings found their way to the surface when Pasquale, her youngest, became an adult. Without her kids consuming her time, the uncertain future was an overwhelming prospect for Arlene. Reversing the mindset of living for others can only come with honest, personal reflection. Interestingly, our low points occurred simultaneously. Just when our hearts needed the most healing, we found each other.

Arlene's beautiful blue eyes had drawn me in, but the comfort we found in each other gave us courage to open our hearts. Also like me, finding comfort in life was always Arlene's greatest desire. We had each spent years putting on a brave face to convince others that things were fine. Despite our best efforts, denying ourselves had been exhausting. In each other, we found the ideal person to fill the void. Arlene and I started to attend Father Ron's occasional healing mass together. Just a few months later, Arlene told me about an intimate—

and revealing—moment she'd shared with her father. He had been living for years with Alzheimer's and was nearing the end of his life. She had gone for a weekend with her siblings to say goodbye. Both of Arlene's parents knew that she had been unhappy, so it was momentous when, just before his passing, Arlene held her father's hand and whispered in his ear that she was happy.

Once I knew I wanted to ask Arlene to marry me, there was no more perfect place than the church where we both found our hearts. I planned everything ahead of time. I asked a former student (who'd become my personal care attendant) and her sister to come to mass and put the ring on my lap when I rolled through communion. I could see them sneaking around and ducking behind people to hide from Arlene. It was a success—they'd stuck the ring box right on my lap. I made my way down the center aisle toward the pulpit. Up to that point, I had been very relaxed, then nerves set in and I started talking to myself. "No big deal. I can do this." I could see my hand shaking slightly on the joystick as I drove the short path back to our spot. I was glad for the moment to get my composure.

The services ended, and the parishioners filed out. I escorted Arlene to the spot where I first prayed to God to heal my heart. My two helpers discreetly filmed the scene with an iPhone. I had Arlene sit down, which she did, then she stood right back up. She had seen the box in my lap and was starting to shake. A smile beamed across her face. Her eyes were more blue that moment than they had ever been before. We were married on a beach in Florida with my parents and cousin, Billy, as witnesses. It was my own romantic movie—a sappy love story, with a poignant engagement, culminating in a wedding on the beach—except, happily, the credits never ran.

A few months later, we hosted a celebration with our families back in Massachusetts. Sharing our love with family and friends was the perfect way to kick off our lives together. Now that I'm married, I am experiencing what I'd only been able to observe with others. A year or so after getting married, I was with my buddies and heard myself say, "You won't believe what my wife did the other day." I realized it was a phrase I'd heard over the years when husbands discussed their wives. Nobody else thought twice about the comment, I'm sure, but that simple exchange—like so many other everyday encounters since I've been married—made me smile. I'd felt different for so long, it was a mini-celebration that life with Arlene now felt authentic. My pillow and my heart are no longer empty.

June 2015. Arlene and I wave to friends and family during our wedding celebration.

CHAPTER 13

Walking Is Overrated

Memories are a great snapshot into the past, but when they start to overtake the present, moving forward in life can be difficult. As his wife, Sandy Chapin, put it in a documentary about Harry Chapin (famous for the song, "Cat's in the Cradle"), "So often, we don't learn life's lessons until it's too late." I shared how much my perspective had changed at the beginning of this book; ironically, breaking my neck forced me to deal with many of life's lessons without warning and every day. Maybe the fact that I don't have control of my hands was to prevent me from holding on to the past. I chose to move forward. Circumstances aside, every human being has the strength to make the same choice, not just to live through our memories, but to motivate ourselves for what comes next. No matter how bleak the outlook, choose to move forward in some way along the path to making new memories. When asked about his favorite Super Bowl, the great philosopher, Tom Brady, always answered, "The next one." I agree with Tom but in a different context. I say, "My favorite memory is the next one."

This sentiment is vastly different from the way I felt many years ago, when I would consider the implications of aging and think, *I don't want to be here when I'm sixty-five.* Now, sixty-five is not far off and doesn't look too bad. Aside from the obvious, I have been lucky to lead a relatively healthy existence to this point. It seems like an oxymoron, like jumbo shrimp, but I'm proud of the fact that I am a healthy quadriplegic. I have always understood how my body works and how to advocate to ensure my medical needs are met. This has allowed me to live life in the manner I desire. Seemingly in a flash, eighteen years old has become fifty-three. I was recently completing an online registration form, when I got to the section about age. For the first time, my age bracket did not have an upper value. I was not in the twenty-five to thirty-five bracket, rather I was farthest right in fifty-one plus. Honestly, I shed a few tears and went to eat some ice cream to feel better.

Aging with SCI is a medical term, but it's basically getting old in a wheelchair. I have about the same function today that I did the day I broke my neck, but after thirty-five years in less-than-ideal circumstances, my body is changing. My blood pressure can drop so low that medical professionals raise their eyebrows when they see the numbers. Medication, hydration, and reclining help relieve low blood pressure when it happens. Something internal is causing discomfort and perspiration related to autonomic dysreflexia. With my lack of feeling, it has been a challenge to diagnose the source, and I spent the last several years sweating as a result. Thankfully, receiving Botox on my bladder paralyzes the nerves and relieves spasticity. I recently found a medication used for seasickness that also relieves spasms in my bowel. The combination of these two treatments has given me relief. (Arlene is also much happier not having to wash sheets and towels filled with my perspiration on a daily basis!)

Even as my body ages, I appreciate that the mental battles I faced were much greater than the physical obstacles along the way. Having self-imposed limits or judgment on my future was not only unrealistic, but personally detrimental. These lessons inspired conversation between a colleague and me one day near the end of my tenure as a math teacher. We were monitoring the intersection of two corridors where students passed between classes. We were outside the Special Education classroom, where teachers and therapists helped students with significant mental or physical disabilities. After the class passed by one afternoon, my colleague shook his head with a sullen face, saying he "felt so bad for those kids." I understood what he meant, and yes, their circumstances were a shame, but I asked him to watch their faces. Indeed, they were often smiling happily. "Those smiles are genuine," I told him. When the bell rang for the rest of the students to switch classes, I suggested he look at their expressions. Few of those kids were smiling. Advantages in life did not necessarily translate to happiness.

Sympathy, to me, suggests pity for a lesser life. I suggested that my colleague consider life from the disabled children's perspectives. They realize they are different, and sadness is a part of their life. Still, you could feel that they were happy whenever you were in their company, and their spirit was contagious. Empathy is understanding why a person may feel as they do, without pity. It's uncomfortable being on the other end of those sympathetic looks. If I don't feel sympathy for myself, I surely don't want it from someone else.

I have been equally uncomfortable being called an inspiration. What does it mean to be an inspiration? Don't you have to do something extraordinary or have some great talent? Tremendous beauty or exceptional intelligence? Taking a bird's eye view of my life, there really isn't much that seems outstanding. I went to college for four years, got a degree in Mathematics Education, and worked for twenty-five years as a high school teacher. I've had my share of volunteer experiences and other accomplishments, but mine is a normal, everyday resume, except, of course, I'm in a wheelchair. This alters some people's perception of me, and I get it—I've had to find my way through extreme adversity. Still, my contributions are no more extraordinary than anybody else's.

This point of view may explain my confusion at being called an inspiration. I have always been gracious, but never comfortable, until an interaction helped me reflect—and accept—what inspiration means. In my twenties and thirties, I often went for rides through our neighborhood in my chair. There was an older woman who lived alone. She had the most beautiful flower garden in the front of her house, which she tended from the first day of spring right through to fall. Her flowers were a symbol of summer for me. I would periodically stop to chat as I was driving by, and she always expressed pride that I was holding down a job while being in a wheelchair, leaving me both appreciative and uncomfortable. Ours was a small but meaningful interaction that I looked forward to each summer.

There came a May that her garden had not been started. Through June, the yard was empty, and I hadn't seen her out at all. It was time to collect donations for the annual Fourth of July BBQ, and my niece and nephew, then five and seven years old, accompanied me to each home in the neighborhood. When we got to my friend's house, the kids knocked on the door. I waited with nervous anticipation. Nobody came to the door, so we rang the bell a second time and started to roll away. A window upstairs opened, and the woman poked her head outside, yelling hello. She explained that she was sick and couldn't get downstairs, but wanted to donate. Two five-dollar bills floated down from the second-floor window. My niece and nephew scurried to put one each in the container and moved on to the next house, while I stayed back for a moment.

"I haven't seen you outside this summer. Your yard doesn't have its usual charm." I smiled up to her.

"It breaks my heart," she acknowledged and explained that she couldn't get down the stairs for gardening, as chemotherapy had made her too tired.

I felt terrible and was so sorry to hear it, which I shared. "The neighborhood isn't the same without your garden."

As I was driving away, she said, "Michael, you are my inspiration."

I remember wondering why someone suffering so much would consider me an inspiration. What was I contributing to society that warranted hearing those words?

We do not decide whom we embolden. People finding inspiration in me is flattering and humbling. I acknowledge that it is not easy to suffer a tragedy and then find one's place in the world. Before writing this book, I always downplayed my accomplishments and personal successes. Though I did very well in school, for example, I was never comfortable putting my report card on the refrigerator. These days, I relish life in Florida, married to beautiful Arlene. I continue to work in education with an online company called Zinkerz, helping high school students from a variety of countries prepare for college entrance exams. I feel similar gratification as I once did in the classroom. A recent thank you letter from a student brought tears to my eyes and warmly validated my intended impact: "Thanks for building my confidence and believing in me. And on top of all, thanks for knowing me. You are much more than a math teacher to me, you are like a life teacher, getting to know all of my problems even without seeing me."

I've already mentioned BACKBONES and the transitional mentor program I directed this past summer for teenagers newly living with a spinal cord injury. Reflecting on my own university experience, it was important to help these kids make the most of their entire college opportunity. We also discussed how to manage and advocate for their own medical care, finding recreation and vacation options that are accessible, and navigating all types of personal relationships. This new undertaking has been a tremendous gift in my life. (Thanks to each one of the participants in the 2022 program for giving me an unforgettable experience. I've documented more thoughts in my blog on the BACKBONES website.)

I still exercise. I have reconfigured my exercise bike to make it stationary—no more baby carriages chasing me down! We continue to travel, something I have always enjoyed. Thankfully, we have many dimensions to our lives. I recently water skied for the first time, and I recognize the accomplishment in it—this wasn't just a regular part of living. It was extraordinary and liberating and exhilarating (thanks to all of the volunteers at Ann's Angels).[2] When I posted my water skiing video on social media, I got a very positive response. I heard again, "Michael, you are an inspiration." For the first time in my life, I am embracing that sentiment.

I have never done anything consciously aimed at being inspirational. In fact, since my injury, I have strived to present myself as no different than anybody else. I recently realized that not embracing my worth goes against every bit of advice or direction that I disseminated to my students over the years. With the kids, I emphasized the need to think of themselves as special and encouraged them to celebrate their accomplishments. I have always found my inspiration

---

[2] Visit Ann's Angels at www.annsangelsawf.org for a video of my water skiing.

in the many lives that have touched mine, and now I finally feel comfortable truly taking my own advice. The moment I hit the boards back in '87, some part of me realized my life would no longer be normal. Living with SCI is, indeed, a challenging existence, as much mentally as it is physically, but great opportunity still exists despite having so much beyond my reach.

May 2021. Arlene and I tearing up the dance floor after we got vaccinated.

EPILOGUE

Sunday, December 3, 2022

I roll down the ramp and take my familiar position next to the pool facing directly southeast. I tilt my chair back and feel the warmth of the sun on my face. The cherry red Mercedes I once dreamt of has been replaced by my shiny blue wheelchair, and that is okay. It seems to me that after I endure something challenging, simple moments become more gratifying.

Lost in my reflection, I am startled when I feel Arlene's arms reach around my neck from behind. She leans in to give me a kiss. Since arriving home from the hospital, her touch feels exponentially better than it did just a few months ago. The time we spent apart intensified by Hurricane Ian has given both of us a greater appreciation for the time we are together. I think back in wonder to when I shied away from human contact.

As she holds me close, I casually mention, "The doctors told me that after eight weeks I can—"

She stops me mid-sentence and pulls away. "Michael, you're injured!" she replies.

This is an aspect of my life that makes many people curious, enough that Arlene sometimes gets questioned, "Can he?" My wife is always uncomfortable responding, so I suggested she have a standard response for whenever she's posed that question: "He's a sexual dynamo!" Obviously, intimacy is a different experience altogether for me. As with most obstacles in my life, I can achieve my goals by adapting with imagination and perseverance.

Arlene's soft hands send electricity throughout my body and give me the most wonderful tingling sensation. The parts of my body that do have feeling are hypersensitive to touch. I can feel the smile on my face. My wife and I are both happy.

I look into those beautiful blue eyes, and I say, "My life is good."

I was energized for many years by the effect I had on people and how I could positively impact the direction of others' lives. In contrast, there have also been times when optimism was hard to come by, but I found my way through by making one simple choice at a time, no matter how difficult. I could never have accomplished anything in my life without assistance, and that's what we all have in common. Being a person in need of help makes you a human being, whether you are standing on two feet or sitting in a chair, and there is a path for every person that chooses to take a step in the right direction. Extraordinary circumstances positioned me to witness the world from two different perspectives, standing and sitting. Now at fifty-three years old, I realize I've achieved what I've been striving for since the first time I sat in a wheelchair thirty-five years ago. A normal life.

MY FAMILY

MY INSPIRATION, MY MOTIVATION, MY JOY!

Diane and Bob   Katelin, Michael, Bachi and Sandra

THIS IS NOT THE CAST OF THE GODFATHER IV, THOUGH THE NAMES MAY REFLECT OTHERWISE.

Santino and Desiree Anthony, Giuliana and Domenic

Micayla and Giovanni   Gianluigi and Aurelia

Janel and Kyle Luca and Genaro   Pasquale

About the Author

Michael R. Maruzzi is a native of Massachusetts, who, in 1987, suffered a devastating injury as a high school hockey player that left him quadriplegic. He went on to earn a bachelor's degree in mathematics at Boston University. Michael enjoyed a rewarding, three-decade career as a high school mathematics teacher, and currently remotely tutors students from all over the world. Michael has been in his wheelchair for over thirty-five years and has authored this memoir to share how each human being has the mental strength and capacity to overcome any physical obstacle.

Michael's most recent accomplishments have included water skiing for the first time and surviving the direct impact of Hurricane Ian. He recently collaborated to develop a peer mentor program for teenagers who have suffered a spinal cord injury. The group discussions were designed to prepare teens for the obstacles and opportunities they may encounter in their journey. Michael now lives in Fort Myers, Florida, with his wife, Arlene and stepson, Pasquale.

CPSIA information can be obtained
at www.ICGtesting.com
Printed in the USA
BVHW052351060723
666783BV00013B/1527

9 798886 444902